Margaret Gee's ~ LOW CHOLESTEROL C U I S I N E

BayBooks

An imprint of HarperCollins*Publishers*

A BAY BOOKS PUBLICATION
An imprint of HarperCollinsPublishers

First published in 1989 in Australia by Bay Books
This edition revised in 1992 by Bay Books, of
CollinsAngus&Robertson Publishers Pty Limited (ACN 009 913 517)
A division of HarperCollinsPublishers (Australia) Pty Limited
25 Ryde Road, Pymble NSW 2073, Australia

HarperCollinsPublishers (New Zealand) Limited
31 View Road, Glenfield, Auckland 10, New Zealand

HarperCollinsPublishers Limited
77-85 Fulham Palace Road, London W6 8JB, United Kingdom

National Library of Australia
Cataloguing-in-Publication data:

Gee, Margaret
    Margaret Gee's low cholesterol cuisine.
    Rev. ed.
    Includes index

    ISBN 1 86378 027 0

    1. Low cholesterol diet - recipes. I. Title.
    (Series: Bay Books cookery collection)

    641.5638

Cover photography by Jon Bader, stying by Donna Hay
Printed in Singapore

5 4 3 2
96 95 94 93 92

CONTENTS

ENJOY LOW CHOLESTEROL EATING

The Chinese have a proverb: food is the first happiness. How right they are. For this book, I have adapted my favourite recipes from around the world to simple lifesaving cooking methods.

Enjoy pasta, spring rolls, moussaka, prawn curry, Mongolian hot pot, falafel, delicious fruit crépes and other favourites from Europe and Asia, knowing that the recipes are based solely on those low cholesterol principles of no added fat, oil, salt or sugar.

The essence of any cuisine lies in the herbs and spices of a particular part of the world, plus the freshest of ingredients. The secret of my preparation techniques is to stir-fry or sauté in a little water or stock. Even those recipes traditionally fried will taste just as delicious oven baked or cooked in a non-stick pan.

My eating program is not about denial. It is about enjoying your food, your health and a wonderfully varied diet based on fresh fruit and vegetables, whole grains and small portions of protein foods.

I have been cooking food this way for many years now, and I know how easy it is to enjoy the style of French cuisine, the charm of an Italian meal or the indulgence of a Chinese banquet — without harmful dietary effects.

This new revised edition provides low fat recipes which everyone can enjoy. Don't forget to take advantage of the new range of low cholesterol, low fat products available in supermarkets. Long may you enjoy your food and your health.

Margaret Gee

LOW CHOLESTEROL BETTER LIVING

If you choose to adopt a low cholesterol diet, you will need to select a variety of foods which satisfy both your enjoyment of eating and your nutritional needs.

If you examine the type of foods you have been consuming for years, you may realise that many are potentially hazardous to your health. Although a healthy diet is highly desirable, it is important not to become fanatical about what you eat, to the extent that you are constantly on guard for 'dangerous' foods.

Good health is a combination of an excellent diet, regular exercise, happy relationships and a positive attitude. Also don't stress yourself by always worrying if you are eating the right or wrong foods.

Once you establish a low cholesterol diet, you gradually get into a pattern of eating correctly, and it is easy to say no to fatty, sugary and salty foods. A low cholesterol diet becomes a self-regulating exercise, as you are no longer inclined towards unhealthy food.

Of course one can't be too pious. Most people on a low fat diet occasionally want to indulge. Once your cholesterol has dropped to a safe level, an occasional breakout is not going to kill you, so don't wallow in guilt if you can't resist temptation.

The best way to demonstrate the value of low cholesterol food is to serve it to any of your sceptical friends or family.

A lifetime of bad eating habits cannot be reversed overnight, and the one sure way to make someone dig in their heels is to nag them. Gradually introduce low fat meals into your family's diet, and you'll soon find their popularity replacing previous family favourites. The days of meat pies, chips and sickly desserts will become a thing of the past.

Best of all, you and your family will be glowing with health.

Above: Strawberry Gelato and Rockmelon Gelato
Far Right: Garlic Prawns
Right: Pizza with Vegetarian Supreme Topping, and Spinach and Ricotta Topping

PANTRY CHECKLIST

Due to increasing consumer demand and awareness a large range of 'Cholesterol Free' and 'Cholesterol Lowered' products are now available in supermarkets. Spend a few extra minutes next time you shop to look for these products as well as salt and sugar-free or reduced products.

DAIRY FOODS
- skim milk
- evaporated skim milk
- condensed skim milk
- low fat yoghurts, plain and fruit-flavoured
- low fat cottage cheese
- fat and salt-reduced cheddar cheese
- fat-reduced mozzarella cheese
- low cholesterol cheese spreads
- fat and salt-reduced fetta
- low fat icecreams
- yolk-free egg mix

CANNED FOODS
- tuna packed in springwater
- salmon packed in springwater
- fat-reduced leg ham
- salt-reduced soups
- vegetables with no added salt such as asparagus, corn and tomatoes
- fruit with no added sugar, packed in natural juice

SAUCES AND CONDIMENTS
- cholesterol-free mayonnaise
- cholesterol-free coleslaw dressing
- oil-free salad dressings e.g. French, Italian
- low salt soy sauce
- tomato sauce with no added salt
- sugar-free jams and fruit spreads

Look out for low fat meats at your delicatessen and for trim cuts of meat at your butcher.

Remember cholesterol-free labels on packets don't mean fat free, so check nutritional analysis and ingredients lists on packaging before buying.

PREPARATION HINTS

- When cooking poultry, remove all skin and visible fat.
- For extra crisp roast vegetables, peel, slice, sprinkle with water and place in the freezer for about 8 minutes. This helps potato and pumpkin in particular to brown and crisp to perfection.
- Low fat yoghurt is a great substitute for cream.
- Line cake tins with baking paper before pouring in mixture. (To take care of non-stick cookware — rinse in hot water or wipe clean with a sponge. Avoid scourers and detergents).
- For barbecues, marinate seafood and meats overnight with salt-reduced soy sauce, dry red or white wine, fruit juice and herbs for flavour.
- Save water used to boil or steam vegetables for soups and sauces. Sprinkle fresh lemon, orange or unsweetened, tinned pineapple juice over any foods which seem too dry.
- Purée fresh fruit in the blender for instant jam.
- Grated Parmesan cheese in small quantities will sharpen up any standard recipe which requires tasty cheese.
- Always preheat a non-stick frypan before adding ingredients, especially for Asian dishes.
- For fresh marmalade: blend together ½ lemon, 1 whole orange and 1 tablespoon of apple juice concentrate.
- Blend raw oats to make a delicious, fine flour. Many nutritional experts believe oats help to keep cholesterol low. Alternatively buy ready-packaged fine or coarse oatmeal.
- When a recipe requires thinly sliced beef, partially freeze beef first for easy slicing.
- For chicken recipes, try turkey breast fillets — they're even leaner than chicken.
- Instead of scooping fatty sour cream into jacket potatoes, spoon on low fat yoghurt and chopped chives — delicious!

SAY YES TO

FRUIT All fresh fruit, frozen fruit and fruit canned in natural juice. Dried fruits are higher in sugar, but are great for cakes and biscuits.

VEGETABLES Eat them in unlimited quantities. Avocados are high in calories but actually cholesterol free. Use for dips or sandwich fillings; half an avocado with a herb dressing is delicious. For spicy guacamole, whip one up with hot chilli and a squeeze of lemon juice.

MEAT, FISH AND CHICKEN Most health experts today advise that fish is the best choice for protein. Moderate quantities of shellfish such as lobster, prawns, oysters and scallops can be included. With any poultry remove all skin and visible fat. Turkey is leaner than chicken. Lean red meat is also fine, but use in moderate quantities.

DRINKS Tea and coffee in moderate quantities. Caffeine is very addictive and too much coffee can make some people anxious or induce insomnia. With either beverage add only skim milk and don't use sugar. If you must use a sweetener, add a small quantity of honey. Mineral water is fine. Only have fruit juices with no added sugar. Stick to freshly made fruit juices.

DAIRY FOODS Use only skim milk, low fat or non-fat yoghurt, and ricotta and cottage cheeses. The hard yellow cheeses are very high in fat, and bries and camemberts are bursting with it. Liven cottage cheese up with crushed garlic, chopped chives, black pepper, chillies, chopped parsley, or chopped spring onions. The occasional sprinkling of Parmesan cheese on Italian food is all right, but remember it is a very salty cheese.

NUTS Most nuts are very high in fat, and many commercial varieties are deep-fried and dipped in salt. Pine nuts and chestnuts can be used.

BREADS, CEREALS, GRAINS Use wholemeal breads not white. Avoid breads that are high in animal fats and salt. Wholemeal crackers are also delicious, but read the labels on the packets carefully. Many crackers are made with animal shortening, which is high in cholesterol. Choose muesli which is low in fat and does not include nuts. Many nutritional experts are now espousing the cholesterol-lowering virtues of oat bran. Robert Kowalski's bestseller, *The 8 Week Cholesterol Cure*, is an excellent book, and oat bran is a major component of his cholesterol-lowering program.

SAY NO TO

ICE CREAM AND CHOCOLATE These are loaded with fat.

CAKES AND BISCUITS These are filled with butter, oil and sugar.

OILS There is much debate about whether or not polyunsaturated oils — safflower and sunflower — and monosaturated oils — such as olive oil — are recommended for a low cholesterol diet. This book does not include oil in the recipes. As you can see, I have

produced more than 200 delectable non-greasy foods without oil, but the choice is yours. Sometimes when I barbecue fish I dribble a small amount of oil onto the hot plate, and grease some cake tins with a little oil to avoid sticking.

FATS Beware of many of the tropical fats — palm oil, cocoa butter and coconut oil — they are very high in cholesterol.

EGGS Egg yolks are out altogether. They are a very concentrated form of cholesterol, but egg whites are completely safe.

SALT Better avoided. There are many natural salts occurring in foods — fruits and vegetables in particular — and it is not necessary to add salt. Many products labelled natural salt or sea salt are also not included in my recipes.

MENUS FOR ALL OCCASIONS

BREAKFAST

The ideal low cholesterol breakfast would include some or all of the following: homemade muesli, raw or cooked; fresh fruit, raw or cooked; egg white scrambled with herbs; wholemeal toast with fruit or cottage cheese spreads; wholemeal pancakes with fruit sauces; fruit juice, coffee or tea (optional).

LUNCH

Lunch suggestions are only limited to your imagination: hot or cold soups; wholemeal open or closed sandwiches; any type of salad, mixed greens with tuna, egg white, tomato, carrot, cucumber, radishes, spring onions, alfalfa sprouts or celery; or a warming slice of spinach pie; spaghetti with zesty pesto sauce; sushi or sashimi; or homemade pizza. If you're really in a hurry, you can't beat a couple of bananas!

DINNER

How often have you heard that variety is the spice of life? You and your family will enjoy eating together more if the meals are varied and tempting. Grilled meat and three vegetables can be enjoyable, but not every night! Mix and match recipes from this exotic international selection and you are sure to delight your family and friends.

For dinner parties, be adventurous. Occasionally forget about a formal sit-down three or four course meal, and cook up a Chinese banquet or an Indian feast. One of the great advantages of Indian food is that most of it, except the rice, can be cooked the previous day. Like good wine, Indian food actually improves with age. The flavours mature, and appetisers such as samosas are even more aromatic the next day.

There is no doubt that a Mongolian Hot Pot party will be an unforgettable experience. Firstly, it is visually spectacular. Your guests will be surrounded by gleaming fresh produce: seafood, lean chicken and meat, crunchy bean sprouts, cabbage, spring onions, luscious noodles and delicious tofu. The process of everyone dipping these tasty morsels into a bubbling stock pot is great fun, and it is a truly delectable and satisfying meal.

If you're thinking of having a barbecue, convert your family and friends from a fatty sausage sizzle to the delights of a seafood or vegetarian barbecue. Chilli Prawns, barbecued fresh corn, Thai-style Grilled Coriander and Garlic Chicken can all make a scrumptious change from traditionally fatty fare.

When cooking Chinese food in a wok, it is easier to cook for four or six, rather than for eight to ten people. However, if you are selective you can present a Chinese banquet for a crowd by choosing dishes which can be cooked earlier and only require reheating at serving time.

Chicken and Sweet Corn Soup, Spring Rolls, Red-cooked Chicken, Beef in Black Bean Sauce, Pineapple Chicken with Tangerine Peel, Szechuan Steamed Eggplant and rice are ideal dinner party choices. In my opinion the essence of a dinner party is to enjoy your guests, so try to select recipes which won't trap you in the kitchen all night.

Probably the most liberating aspect of low cholesterol cuisine is that when it comes to desserts the simplest solution is seasonal, well ripened fruit attractively presented on a platter. Occasionally it is fun to create a mouth-watering dessert such as Ricotta Cake, Pisa Peaches, or Pineapple Cake, but no one will mind if you serve fresh mangoes!

Chicken Tonkatsu

Minestrone Soup

EUROPEAN CLASSICS

A selection of delicious, healthy dishes to silence the critics and encourage the cautious. These gastronomic delights are as good for you as they are quick to prepare and satisfying to eat. All in all, you will be amazed at the variety of delicious and simple recipes in this chapter, which are healthy and low cholesterol too!

The health revolution has finally caught up with the French and, mercifully, it is now possible to delight in French food not swimming in butter, cream, oil, salt, sugar and egg yolks.

Not all Italian food contains olive oil, Parmesan cheese, olives, butter and cream. Pasta, pizza, risotto, minestrone, gelato and many other irresistible Italian treats can be prepared using low fat, low cholesterol ingredients.

There is more to British food than pork pies, steak and kidney pudding, treacle tart, peas and chips. Try my adaptations of traditional favourites like Shepherd's Pie and Cock-a-Leekie.

Greece is fascinating, whether you're digging for ancient ruins or edible treats. Each region offers specialities which are hard to resist.

Middle Eastern cuisine is wonderful and surprisingly simple to prepare. Traditional dishes often include lamb, but you can substitute lean beef, chicken, fish or vegetables.

Country Beef Terrine and Salad Niçoise

*The following recipes
belong to a style sometimes
called Cuisine Naturelle.
They make full use of the
wonderful Gallic ability
to turn a basic meal of
bread, salad, fruit and
wine into an occasion.*

CUISINE NATURELLE

FRENCH ONION SOUP

7 cups (1¾ litres) beef or vegetable stock

4 medium-sized white onions, thinly sliced

1 clove garlic, chopped

1 tablespoon wholemeal flour

½ cup (125 ml) dry white wine

1 bay leaf

freshly ground black pepper

2 teaspoons finely chopped fresh parsley

CHEESE CROUTONS

1 cup fresh ricotta or low fat cottage cheese

2 tablespoons Parmesan cheese

freshly ground black pepper

4 slices wholemeal thick-sliced bread

1 Bring 2 cups (500 ml) stock to the boil.
Add onions and garlic, cover and simmer for
20 minutes. Mix flour with a little water to
form a smooth paste and add to saucepan.
Stir and cook for a further 2 minutes.

French Onion Soup

2 Add remaining stock with wine, bay leaf
and pepper. Bring to the boil, cover and
simmer slowly for 40 minutes. Occasionally
skim surface.

3 TO MAKE CROUTONS: Preheat oven to
190°C (375°F). Mash cheeses with pepper
and spread on to toast slices. Cut into small
squares or round shapes, and bake for
20 minutes. To serve, ladle out soup and top
with croutons and chopped parsley.

SERVES 4 TO 6

PARISIAN FISH SOUP

8 cups (2 litres) fish stock

½ cup (125 ml) white wine

300 g very ripe tomatoes, seeded and diced

1 clove garlic, chopped

1 teaspoon grated orange zest

**½ fresh red chilli, finely chopped and seeds
removed**

3 sprigs fresh parsley, chopped

1 sprig fresh thyme

1 to 2 saffron threads

750 g fish fillets, cut into large chunks

**250 g uncooked (green) prawns, shelled
and deveined**

10 mussels, thoroughly cleaned

extra chopped, fresh parsley, for garnish

1 Place stock, wine, tomatoes, garlic,
orange zest, chilli, parsley, thyme and saffron
in a large saucepan. Bring to the boil.
Reduce heat, cover and simmer for
20 minutes. Strain through a fine sieve.

2 Bring liquid to the boil again and add
fish chunks. Reduce heat, cover and simmer
for 3 to 4 minutes.

3 Add prawns and mussels and simmer for a
further 3 to 4 minutes. Discard any mussels
that don't open. Garnish with parsley and
serve with wholemeal Pritikin bread.

SERVES 4 TO 6

VICHYSSOISE

4 cups (1 litre) chicken stock

1 white onion, sliced

4 leeks, white part only, chopped and well washed

1 tablespoon chopped, fresh parsley

1 stalk celery and 2 leaves, chopped

3 medium-sized potatoes, thinly sliced

freshly ground black pepper

½ cup (125 ml) skim milk

1 Bring ½ cup (125 ml) stock to the boil and add onion and leeks. Cover and simmer for 5 minutes.

2 Add remaining stock, parsley, celery, potatoes and pepper and simmer for 20 minutes.

3 Cool, then purée and stir in skim milk. Chill and serve.

Serves 4 to 6

CRUDITES

2 stalks celery, sliced diagonally

4 carrots, peeled and sliced

100 g cauliflower, separated into florets

8 radishes, trimmed

1 red capsicum (pepper), sliced in thin strips

1 green capsicum (pepper), sliced in thin strips

4 spring onions, trimmed and cut into short lengths

100 g butternut pumpkin, cut into curls with potato peeler

100 g zucchini, trimmed and sliced

alfalfa sprouts, for garnish

1 Arrange the vegetables attractively, garnish with alfalfa sprouts and serve with your favourite dressing.

Serves 4 to 6

SALMON MOUSSE

420 g canned red salmon, well drained

1 tablespoon white wine vinegar

1 tablespoon gelatine

¼ cup (60 ml) boiling water

125 g ricotta cheese combined with 1 tablespoon skim milk

2 teaspoons tomato paste

½ cup finely chopped celery

4 spring onions, finely chopped

1 tablespoon cucumber, peeled, seeded and finely chopped

2 teaspoons chopped fresh dill

1 teaspoon cayenne pepper

freshly ground black pepper

1 Blend salmon with vinegar until smooth.

2 Mix gelatine with water and dissolve. Stir ricotta and milk mixture into gelatine and water. Stir into blended salmon.

3 Add tomato paste, celery, spring onions, cucumber, dill and peppers. Mix until well combined.

4 Pour into a glass mould or dish. Cover and chill overnight. Unmould carefully and serve with crudites (see recipe).

Serves 4 to 6

SALMON RICE SALAD WITH PERNOD

3 eggs, hard-boiled

210 g canned salmon (water-packed)

1 head fennel, thinly sliced

½ cup (125 ml) low fat yoghurt

2 spring onions, thinly sliced

3 cups cooked brown rice

1 teaspoon chopped, fresh dill

squeeze fresh lemon juice

1 teaspoon Pernod

freshly ground black pepper

1 Discard egg yolks and chop whites only. Combine all ingredients, chill and serve.

Serves 4 to 6

SALADE NIÇOISE

3 hard-boiled eggs

1 lettuce

1 bunch curly endive

3 tomatoes, sliced

150 g green beans, trimmed and slightly steamed

200 g new potatoes, steamed and diced

1 green capsicum (pepper), thinly sliced

425 g canned tuna (water-packed)

2 tablespoons chopped, fresh parsley

DRESSING

1 cup (250 ml) unsweetened orange juice

2 teaspoons white wine vinegar

1 teaspoon finely chopped, fresh basil

1 clove garlic, finely chopped

freshly ground black pepper

1 Discard egg yolks and slice whites.

2 Arrange salad ingredients in a bowl or on a platter.

3 Mix together dressing ingredients and pour over salad.

SERVES 4 TO 6

RATATOUILLE

1 medium-sized eggplant (aubergine), cubed

2 white onions, thinly sliced

2 cloves garlic, finely chopped

2 medium-sized zucchini (courgette), sliced

2 very ripe medium-sized tomatoes, sliced

1 tablespoon tomato paste, mixed with 1 cup (250 ml) water

freshly ground black pepper

1 red capsicum (pepper), sliced

2 sprigs fresh parsley

1 sprig fresh thyme

1 Place eggplant cubes on absorbent paper for 20 minutes to absorb bitter juices. Rinse and pat dry.

2 Combine all ingredients except parsley and thyme. Bring to the boil, reduce heat and simmer for 15 minutes.

3 Add parsley and thyme, simmer for an extra 5 minutes. Serve with wholemeal bread.

SERVES 4 TO 6

TARRAGON CHICKEN

1 white onion

1½ kg chicken, skinned

½ cup (125 ml) chicken stock

2 tablespoons finely chopped, fresh tarragon or 2 teaspoons dried tarragon

3 sprigs fresh parsley

freshly ground black pepper

1 Preheat oven to 200°C (400°F).

2 Place onion inside cavity of chicken. Pour chicken stock over chicken and sprinkle it with other ingredients.

3 Place in an ovenproof dish and cover with foil. Bake for 15 minutes, then reduce heat to 180°C (350°F) and bake for another hour.

4 Remove foil and cook for a further 15 minutes until chicken is brown. Baste with pan juices during cooking.

SERVES 4 TO 6

COUNTRY BEEF TERRINE

2 medium-sized carrots, chopped

1 medium-sized white onion, chopped

1 medium-sized green capsicum (pepper)

2 cloves garlic, chopped

1 tablespoon chopped, fresh rosemary or 1 teaspoon dried rosemary

500 g lean minced beef

freshly ground black pepper

1 tablespoon dry white wine

1 egg white

1 cup homemade breadcrumbs

1 tablespoon tomato paste

1 Blend all vegetables, garlic and rosemary. Add to meat with pepper, wine, egg white, breadcrumbs and tomato paste. Mix until well combined.

2 Spoon into a 28 cm x 10 cm lined or non-stick loaf tin. and bake for 1 hour. Remove from tin and allow to cool. Wrap and refrigerate.

SERVES 4 TO 6

RIVIERA PAELLA

150 g squid, cleaned

¾ cup (185 ml) chicken stock

2 cloves garlic, chopped

1 white onion, chopped

4 ripe medium-sized tomatoes, chopped

3 tablespoons tomato paste

2 chicken breasts, trimmed of all visible fat and chopped into small pieces

½ red capsicum (pepper), diced

1 teaspoon paprika

2 pinches saffron threads

freshly ground black pepper

1 kg firm fish fillets, cut into chunks

125 g shelled fresh peas

200 g uncooked (green) prawns, shelled and deveined, tails left on

1½ cups (375 ml) dry white wine

12 uncooked mussels in their shells, trimmed and well scrubbed

6 cups cooked brown rice

lemon wedges, for garnish

1 Cut squid into rings and cook in boiling water to cover for 5 minutes. Drain and set aside.

2 Preheat a large non-stick frypan and add chicken stock. Bring to the boil and add garlic, onion, tomatoes and tomato paste. Simmer in stock for 2 to 3 minutes.

3 Add chicken pieces and red capsicum and stir-fry for a further 8 minutes.

4 Add paprika, saffron, pepper, fish pieces and peas. Simmer for 5 minutes.

5 Top with prawns and wine and continue simmering for a further 3 to 4 minutes. Add mussels and squid and simmer for another 2 minutes. Discard any mussels which remain tightly closed.

6 Carefully remove everything from pan. Place cooked brown rice in pan and heat through with small amount of pan juices. Return paella mixture to pan on top of rice. Simmer for a further 2 to 3 minutes. Add a little extra water or dash of wine if necessary.

Riviera Paella

7 Serve garnished with lemon wedges. It is usual to bring the paella pan to the table for people to help themselves.

SERVES 4 TO 6

❧ PAELLA

Paella is traditionally a Spanish dish, but is found all along the French coast. Small portions of chicken, rabbit and even snails are sometimes added to French paellas. This recipe is great fun for a dinner party. Use your largest frypan and, if you think you are going to be a regular paella eater, buy a massive Spanish paella pan.

COQ AU VIN

1 cup (250 ml) water

2 onions, chopped

2 cloves garlic, finely chopped

1½ kg chicken, skinned and cut into pieces

1 heaped tablespoon wholemeal flour

2 bay leaves

2 carrots, sliced

2 very ripe tomatoes, chopped

2 teaspoons tomato paste

2 cups (500 ml) red wine

freshly ground black pepper

1 tablespoon chopped, fresh parsley

200 g button mushrooms, halved

1 Place water in a large saucepan and bring to the boil. Add onions and garlic. Cover and simmer for 5 minutes.

2 Sprinkle chicken pieces with flour and add to saucepan with bay leaves. Reduce heat, cover and simmer for 5 minutes.

3 Add all other ingredients except parsley and mushrooms. Cover and simmer slowly for 35 minutes.

4 Add mushrooms and simmer for a further 5 minutes. Stir through chopped parsley and serve.

SERVES 4 TO 6

CHICKEN AND PEACH TERRINE

1 kg chicken fillets, skinned and trimmed of any visible fat

1 ripe golden peach or 1 cup well-drained peaches in natural juice

1 tablespoon chopped fresh herbs (sage, oregano, thyme) or 1 teaspoon dried herbs

1 onion, chopped

1 carrot, chopped

1 egg white, lightly beaten

squeeze fresh lemon juice

1 cup homemade breadcrumbs

freshly ground black pepper

1 Preheat oven to 190°C (375°F).

2 Mince chicken in blender, remove and set aside.

3 Peel peach and remove stone. (If using canned variety, dry peaches in a clean tea towel.) Blend peach, herbs, onion and carrot.

4 Add to chicken mince. Combine with egg white, lemon juice, breadcrumbs and pepper.

5 Spoon into a 28 cm x 10 cm lined or non-stick loaf tin and bake for 45 minutes. This dish tastes best eaten cold the next day.

SERVES 4 TO 6

STEAK WITH PEPPER SAUCE

4 small steaks (fillet or rump), trimmed of all visible fat

½ cup (125 ml) dry sherry

finely chopped, fresh parsley for garnish

SAUCE

1¼ cups (310 ml) beef or chicken stock

1 tablespoon white onion, finely chopped

2 tablespoons cornflour

2 teaspoons freshly ground black pepper

1 teaspoon brandy

pinch hot paprika

1 Marinate steak in sherry for at least 2 hours.

2 **TO MAKE SAUCE:** Bring ½ cup (125 ml) stock to the boil. Add onion, cover and simmer for 3 minutes.

3 Mix cornflour with remaining stock. Add to saucepan with pepper, brandy and sherry marinade. Simmer and stir for 2 to 3 minutes. Stir in paprika. Set aside and keep warm.

4 Grill steaks until tender (5 to 10 minutes each side, depending on thickness). Pour over sauce, garnish with parsley and serve.

SERVES 4 TO 6

STEP-BY-STEP TECHNIQUES

OAT CRÊPES WITH PEACHES AND RASPBERRY COULIS

4 peaches, sliced and stones removed

2 tablespoons Cointreau

CRÊPES

1 cup (125 g) wholemeal plain flour

1 cup (155 g) fine oatmeal

½ teaspoon mixed spice

1 egg white

2 cups (500 ml) skim milk

RASPBERRY COULIS

300 g fresh or frozen raspberries

2 teaspoons fresh lemon juice

TO SERVE

1 cup (250 ml) low fat vanilla yoghurt, whipped

1 Place peaches in a bowl with Cointreau, set aside.

2 TO MAKE CRÊPES: Combine flour, oatmeal, mixed spice, egg white and milk, and mix until smooth.

3 Preheat a non-stick frypan to very hot. Pour a little of the crépe mixture into the pan and rotate until crépe spreads into a circle. Cook until bubbles appear, then turn over with non-stick spatula and cook other side.

4 TO MAKE RASPBERRY COULIS: Blend raspberries roughly and stir through lemon juice.

5 Serve each person a stack of 2 to 3 crépes, folded on the plate. Top with raspberry coulis and garnish with peaches and a dollop of yoghurt.

SERVES 6 TO 8

Combine flour, oatmeal, mixed spice, egg white and milk and mix until smooth.

Cook crépes in a preheated frypan until bubbles appear then turn over with a spatula.

For the coulis, press raspberries through a sieve or blend roughly.

ITALIAN CUISINE

SPINACH SOUP

1 bunch fresh spinach, with stalks removed

2 cloves garlic, chopped

1 medium-sized onion, thinly sliced

3 cups (750 ml) vegetable stock

1½ cups (375 ml) skim milk

½ cup chopped, fresh parsley

1 teaspoon freshly grated nutmeg

freshly ground black pepper

1 Wash and finely chop spinach.

2 Place garlic and onion in a large saucepan with 2 cups (500 ml) stock. Simmer covered for 5 minutes.

3 Add all other ingredients except nutmeg and pepper. Simmer for 20 minutes.

4 Purée half the soup and return it to saucepan. Stir in nutmeg and pepper. Simmer for 5 minutes and serve.

SERVES 4 TO 6

Minestrone Soup

MINESTRONE SOUP

2 medium-sized onions, thinly sliced

2 cloves garlic, finely chopped

4 cups (1 litre) chicken, beef or vegetable stock

1 cup finely chopped celery

3 carrots, thinly sliced

2 zucchini (courgettes), finely chopped

3 very ripe tomatoes, finely chopped

3 tablespoons tomato paste

3 cups cooked, dried beans (borlotti or cannellini)

2 tablespoons finely chopped, fresh oregano or 2 teaspoons dried oregano

1 cup cooked brown rice

freshly ground black pepper

1 Place onions and garlic in a large saucepan with 2 cups (500 ml) stock. Simmer covered for 5 minutes.

2 Add all other ingredients to saucepan except oregano, rice and pepper. Simmer covered for 30 minutes.

3 Purée half the soup and return it to the saucepan. Add oregano, rice and pepper, and simmer for 8 minutes. Serve hot with wholemeal bread.

SERVES 4 TO 6

PAVAROTTI POTATO AND ONION SOUP

5 medium-sized onions, thinly sliced

2 cloves garlic, finely chopped

4 cups (1 litre) chicken, beef or vegetable stock

8 medium-sized potatoes, roughly chopped

1 cup (250 ml) skim milk

freshly ground black pepper

finely chopped, fresh parsley, for garnish

1 Place onions and garlic in a large saucepan with 2 cups (500 ml) stock. Simmer covered for 5 minutes.

2 Add all remaining ingredients and simmer for 30 minutes. Purée and serve, garnished with parsley.

SERVES 4 TO 6

Fennel has the flavour of aniseed. Its leaves are used as a herb and its seeds are also used to add flavour to food such as breads and pastries. Fennel should stored in a plastic bag in the fridge.

FENNEL SALAD

2 large fennel bulbs
1 cucumber, thinly sliced
1 red capsicum (pepper), sliced
1 small onion, thinly sliced

DRESSING

1 cup (250 ml) fresh orange juice
1 teaspoon red or white wine vinegar
1 tablespoon chopped, fresh mint
freshly ground black pepper

1 Remove outer leaves from fennel bulbs and slice the bulbs finely. Mix with other salad vegetables.

2 Combine dressing ingredients and leave in refrigerator for 30 minutes. Pour over salad just before serving.

SERVES 4 TO 6

MIXED ITALIAN SALAD

2 crisp mignonette lettuce
1 radicchio
1 green capsicum (pepper), thinly sliced
1 red capsicum (pepper), thinly sliced
2 medium-sized tomatoes, sliced
½ cucumber, thinly sliced
1 clove garlic, finely chopped
8 radishes, thinly sliced

DRESSING

1 cup (250 ml) fresh orange juice
squeeze fresh lemon juice
2 teaspoons red or white wine vinegar
1 tablespoon finely chopped, fresh parsley
freshly ground black pepper

1 Rinse, drain and tear up lettuce leaves and radicchio.

2 Place all salad ingredients in a bowl.

3 Combine dressing ingredients and marinate in refrigerator for 30 minutes. Pour over salad just before serving.

SERVES 4 TO 6

MUSHROOMS WITH GARLIC

500 g button mushrooms, thinly sliced
3 cloves garlic, finely chopped
1 red onion, finely chopped
2 tablespoons white wine vinegar
2 tablespoons fresh orange juice
2 tablespoons finely chopped, fresh parsley, for garnish

1 Combine all ingredients and allow to stand for 1 hour. Serve as a cold entrée or appetiser.

SERVES 4 TO 6

EGGPLANT AND TOMATO BAKE

1 kg medium-sized eggplants (aubergine), thinly sliced
4 very ripe medium-sized tomatoes, sliced
2 tablespoons finely chopped, fresh oregano or 2 teaspoons dried oregano
1 tablespoon finely chopped, fresh parsley
1 tablespoon tomato paste
1 cup (250 ml) dry white wine
300 g fresh ricotta cheese
2 tablespoons grated Parmesan cheese
1½ cups wholemeal breadcrumbs
freshly ground black pepper

1 Preheat oven to 200°C (400°F).

2 Place eggplant slices on kitchen paper for 20 minutes. Rinse and pat dry.

3 Layer alternately with tomato slices in medium-sized oven-proof dish. Sprinkle with oregano and parsley.

4 Mix tomato paste with white wine and pour over.

5 Combine ricotta and Parmesan cheese with breadcrumbs and spoon on top. Sprinkle with pepper and bake for 40 minutes until brown on top.

SERVES 4 TO 6

STUFFED TOMATOES

8 very ripe medium-sized tomatoes

1 medium-sized onion, finely chopped

1 clove garlic, finely chopped

¼ cup (60 ml) water

½ green or red capsicum (pepper), finely chopped

2 cups cooked brown rice

1 tablespoon finely chopped, fresh basil or 1 teaspoon dried basil

1 tablespoon finely chopped, fresh parsley

250 g fresh ricotta cheese

2 tablespoons grated Parmesan cheese

1 Preheat oven to 180°C (350°F).

2 Slice the top off each tomato and set aside the tops. Scoop out tomato flesh and chop. Reserve tomato cases.

3 Simmer onion and garlic in water for 5 minutes. Combine with all remaining ingredients and mix well.

4 Drain off excess liquid and spoon mixture into tomato cases. Put tomato tops back and place on a non-stick baking tray. Bake for 15 minutes and serve.

SERVES 4 TO 6

TUSCAN TOMATOES

8 medium-sized tomatoes, sliced

1 tablespoon finely chopped, fresh oregano or 1 teaspoon dried oregano

1 clove garlic, finely chopped

1 cup (250 ml) unsweetened orange juice

1 teaspoon red wine vinegar

freshly ground black pepper

1 Mix all ingredients together, chill and serve as a cold entrée or appetiser.

SERVES 4 TO 6

STUFFED ZUCCHINI

8 medium-sized zucchini (courgettes)

1 cup homemade wholemeal breadcrumbs

1 tablespoon finely chopped, fresh oregano or 1 teaspoon dried oregano

1 clove garlic, finely chopped

1 small onion, finely chopped

freshly ground black pepper

250 g fresh ricotta cheese

1 Preheat oven to 200°C (400°F).

2 Bring a large saucepan of water to the boil. Plunge zucchini in for 2 minutes and drain in colander. Cut in half lengthways and scoop out flesh. Set aside.

3 Mix breadcrumbs, oregano, garlic, onion, pepper and ricotta cheese until mixture is crumbly. Mix in zucchini flesh.

4 Stuff mixture back into zucchini shells and bake for 20 minutes.

SERVES 4 TO 6

HERBED POTATO CROQUETTES

1 kg potatoes, boiled and mashed

2 cloves garlic, finely chopped

100 g fresh ricotta cheese

2 tablespoons grated Parmesan cheese

1 tablespoon finely chopped, fresh oregano or 1 teaspoon dried oregano

1 tablespoon finely chopped, fresh basil or 1 teaspoon dried basil

freshly ground black pepper

3 egg whites, lightly beaten

2 cups homemade wholemeal breadcrumbs

1 Preheat oven to 200°C (400°F).

2 Combine mashed potato, garlic, ricotta and Parmesan cheese, herbs and pepper.

3 Roll mixture into small balls. Dip into egg whites and coat firmly with breadcrumbs. Bake for 30 minutes or until brown.

SERVES 4 TO 6

✎ READY-TO-USE GARLIC

Blend some garlic cloves with a little white vinegar and store in the fridge in an airtight jar. Use whenever crushed or chopped garlic is required in a recipe.

❧ HOW TO COOK AND SERVE PASTA

It is important to use a large saucepan or soup pot. For 1 kg of pasta use a minimum of 8 cups (4 litres) of water. Wait until the water is boiling furiously, then drop in the pasta. If you are using long strands of pasta — spaghetti, fettucine, tagliatelle — bend the pasta into the water. Don't break it up.

It is hard to estimate exactly how long to cook pasta. You must test it yourself to see when it is 'al dente' — firm to the bite. Fresh pasta cooks quickly: 2 to 4 minutes; dried pasta takes 10 to 12 minutes; and filled pasta (such as ravioli or tortellini) 10 minutes. Cooked pasta should never be deluged with cold water and drained.

I think it is much better to mix the sauce in with the pasta before you serve it. If you pass the sauce round, by the time everyone has been served, the pasta will be cold.

Pasta with Tomato and
Basil Sauce

TOMATO SAUCE

1 medium-sized onion, thinly sliced
3 cloves garlic, finely chopped
1 cup (250 ml) water
500 g fresh ripe tomatoes, roughly chopped
1 tablespoon tomato paste
freshly ground black pepper

1 Place onion, garlic and water in a saucepan. Cover and simmer for 5 minutes.
2 Add all other ingredients, cover and simmer for 10 minutes. Purée and serve with freshly cooked pasta.
3 Alternatively, you can blend the above ingredients, heat through and serve if you want an 'instant' sauce.
SERVES 4

TOMATO AND BASIL SAUCE

1 medium-sized onion, thinly sliced
3 cloves garlic
1 cup (250 ml) water
500 g very ripe tomatoes
freshly ground black pepper
1 bunch fresh basil, roughly chopped, with stalks removed

1 Place onion, garlic and water in a saucepan. Cover and simmer for 5 minutes.
2 Add tomatoes and pepper, cover and simmer for 10 minutes.
3 Purée, stir in basil and serve.
SERVES 4

GARLIC AND PARSLEY SAUCE

10 cloves garlic, finely chopped
1 cup finely chopped, fresh parsley
1 cup (250 ml) unsweetened orange juice
squeeze fresh lemon juice
freshly ground black pepper

1 Blend all ingredients and mix through freshly cooked pasta.
SERVES 4

CHILLI SAUCE

500 g very ripe tomatoes

1 medium-sized onion, finely chopped

1 tablespoon tomato paste

**2 fresh red or green chillies, chopped
and seeds removed**

½ cup (125 ml) water

freshly ground black pepper

1 Place all ingredients in a saucepan and simmer, covered, for 10 minutes.

2 Purée, and serve with freshly cooked pasta.

SERVES 4

TOMATO AND LEMON SAUCE

1 cup (250 ml) fresh lemon juice

500 g very ripe tomatoes

1 tablespoon tomato paste

1 clove garlic, chopped

freshly ground black pepper

1 Place all ingredients in a saucepan and simmer, covered, for 10 minutes.

2 Purée, simmer for a further 5 minutes and serve with freshly cooked pasta.

SERVES 4

MUSHROOM AND RICOTTA SAUCE

300 g fresh ricotta cheese

1 cup (250 ml) skim milk

2 cloves garlic, finely chopped

freshly ground black pepper

300 g fresh button mushrooms, sliced

finely chopped, fresh parsley, for garnish

1 Purée ricotta cheese with skim milk, garlic and black pepper.

2 Stir in sliced mushrooms. Garnish with parsley.

SERVES 4

BOLOGNESE SAUCE

400 g lean minced beef

1 cup (250 ml) water

1 clove garlic, finely chopped

1 medium-sized onion, thinly sliced

1 tablespoon tomato paste

1 cup diced celery

1 medium-sized carrot, diced

**1 tablespoon chopped, fresh oregano or
1 teaspoon dried oregano**

1½ cups (375 ml) dry white wine

**3 ripe medium-sized tomatoes,
roughly chopped**

freshly ground black pepper

1 Place beef, water, garlic and onion in a non-stick frypan. Cover and simmer for 5 minutes.

2 Add the remaining ingredients and simmer, covered, for 30 minutes. Serve with freshly cooked pasta.

SERVES 4

PESTO SAUCE

I think this sauce is the pesto de resistance! It is light, zesty and 'different'.

**1 large bunch fresh basil, with
stalks removed (dried basil is not an option
if you want the real thing)**

6 cloves garlic, chopped

½ cup pine nuts (optional)

300 g fresh ricotta cheese

¾ cup (185 ml) skim milk

freshly ground black pepper

1 Mash all ingredients in a mortar and pestle, or blend together. Mix through freshly cooked pasta.

SERVES 4

❧ PASTA PER PERSON

As a general guide, 100 g of uncooked pasta per person is sufficient for a main course.

Chicken Cacciatore

SPINACH LASAGNE

1 bay leaf

1 large bunch fresh spinach, stalks removed

250 g spinach or wholemeal lasagne sheets (about 12)

500 g fresh ricotta cheese

2 tablespoons grated Parmesan cheese

2½ cups wholemeal breadcrumbs

4 very ripe medium-sized tomatoes, thinly sliced

1 medium-sized onion, finely chopped

2 cloves garlic, finely chopped

1 tablespoon finely chopped, fresh basil or 1 teaspoon dried basil

1 tablespoon finely chopped, fresh oregano or 1 teaspoon dried oregano

2 tablespoons tomato paste, mixed with 1½ cups (375 ml) water or vegetable stock

freshly ground black pepper

1 teaspoon freshly grated nutmeg

1 Preheat oven to 200°C (400°F).

2 Place bay leaf in a large saucepan of water and bring to the boil. Drop in spinach leaves for 1 minute. Remove, drain well, chop finely and set aside.

3 Bring a large saucepan of water to the boil. Drop in lasagne sheets, 3 at a time. Cook for 10 to 12 minutes until tender. Plunge into cold water, drain and set aside.

4 Mix ricotta and Parmesan cheese with breadcrumbs until mixture is crumbly, and divide into 4 portions.

5 Layer a 30 cm x 20 cm non-stick baking dish in the following order:

- 4 lasagne sheets
- portion of breadcrumb mixture
- spinach
- tomatoes
- onion and garlic
- basil and oregano

Repeat the process three times and top with a layer of lasagne sheets.

6 Pour tomato paste and water mixture over the top. Sprinkle with remaining ricotta, Parmesan and breadcrumb mixture. Season with pepper and sprinkle with nutmeg. Bake for 40 minutes until top is brown.

SERVES 4 TO 6

CHICKEN CACCIATORE

1½ kg chicken, skinned, trimmed of all visible fat and cut into 6 pieces

1 medium-sized onion, thinly sliced

3 cloves garlic, finely chopped

1½ cups (375 ml) dry white wine

4 very ripe medium-sized tomatoes, roughly chopped

1 tablespoon tomato paste

1 bay leaf

freshly ground black pepper

finely chopped, fresh parsley, for garnish

1 Place all ingredients except parsley in a large saucepan. Cover and simmer for 40 minutes until chicken is tender. The gravy can be thickened with 2 teaspoons wholemeal flour mixed with cold water and added to the pan.

2 Remove bay leaf, garnish with parsley.

SERVES 4 TO 6

🐚 **LASAGNE**

You can buy lasagne that does not need to be pre-boiled. Always check the packet to make sure.

RICOTTA CAKE

BASE

1 cup (90 g) raw oats, blended into coarse crumbs

1 teaspoon freshly grated nutmeg

3 tablespoons apple juice concentrate

FILLING

1 cup (155 g) currants, marinated in ½ cup (125 ml) marsala for 30 minutes

500 g fresh ricotta cheese, well drained

2 egg whites

1 tablespoon finely grated lemon zest

1 tablespoon finely grated orange zest

1 tablespoon gelatine mixed with 2 tablespoons hot water

½ teaspoon vanilla essence

1 Combine base ingredients and press into the bottom of a non-stick dish. Refrigerate for 1 hour.

2 Preheat oven to 180°C (375°F).

3 Remove currants from marsala and drain. Add currants to other filling ingredients. Beat or blend until smooth and creamy. Pour into 20 cm dish and bake for 40 minutes. Cool, refrigerate, slice and serve.

SERVES 4 TO 6

PISA PEACHES

1 cup pine nuts

1 cup (155 g) currants

1 teaspoon cinnamon

4 fresh golden peaches, halved and stoned

2 cups (500 ml) marsala

1 Preheat oven to 180°C (375°F).

2 Blend together pine nuts, currants and cinnamon. Stuff blended mixture into cavity of each peach half.

3 Place peaches cut side up in non-stick baking dish and pour marsala over them. Bake for 25 minutes and serve.

SERVES 4

Strawberry Gelato and Rockmelon Gelato

STRAWBERRY GELATO

4 cups fresh strawberries, hulled and puréed

1 cup (250 ml) water

1 cup (250 ml) lemon juice

1 tablespoon gelatine mixed with 2 tablespoons boiling water

1 Add all other ingredients and blend or beat until well combined. Pour into icecream trays and freeze for 2 hours.

2 Remove from freezer, blend until smooth and re-freeze. Remove from freezer 5 minutes before serving.

SERVES 4 TO 6

ᔊ ROCKMELON GELATO

For Rockmelon Gelato, substitute 1 medium-sized rockmelon, peeled, seeded and puréed, for strawberries.

THE BEST OF BRITISH

SCOTCH BROTH

1 cup (250 ml) water

1 large onion, sliced

1 leek, white part only, thinly sliced

8 cups (2 litres) beef or vegetable stock

1 cup fresh peas

3 carrots, grated

1 turnip, diced

¼ cup diced celery

½ small cabbage, finely shredded

1 cup pearl barley

freshly ground black pepper

500 g beef or lamb fillet, trimmed of all visible fat and thinly sliced

¼ cup finely chopped, fresh parsley

1 In a saucepan bring water to the boil, add onion and leek. Reduce heat, cover and simmer for 5 minutes.

2 Add all other ingredients except beef and parsley. Bring to the boil, reduce heat, cover and simmer for 15 minutes.

3 Add beef slices and simmer for another 30 minutes on a low heat. Stir in chopped parsley. Heat through and serve with wholemeal Pritikin bread.

SERVES 4 TO 6

🐦 **THINLY SLICED BEEF**

When a recipe requires thinly sliced beef, partially freeze the beef first and it will be much easier to slice.

PEASE PUDDING

2½ cups (500 g) split peas, yellow or green

1 onion, thinly sliced

1 bay leaf

freshly ground black pepper

1 egg white

2 teaspoons finely chopped, fresh parsley

1 Rinse split peas well. Cover with water and soak overnight. Rinse and drain.

2 Cover soaked peas with 2½ cups (625 ml) water. Add onion, bay leaf and pepper. Bring to the boil, cover and simmer for 1¼ hours. Remove lid and simmer for a further 15 minutes.

3 Stir through egg white and parsley and heat through. Purée and serve.

SERVES 4 TO 6

TATTY POT

1 cup (250 ml) water

2 white onions, thinly sliced

1 cup cottage cheese

2 tablespoons grated Parmesan cheese

1½ cups (375 ml) skim milk

1 kg potatoes, peeled and thinly sliced

1 teaspoon dried sage

freshly ground black pepper

1 Preheat oven to 190°C (375°F).

2 Bring water to the boil in a saucepan and add onions. Reduce heat, cover and simmer for 5 minutes. Drain and set aside.

3 Purée cottage and Parmesan cheese with skim milk. Combine well with onions.

4 Layer potatoes in a large ovenproof dish. Pour over cheese, milk and onion mixture. Sprinkle with dried sage and pepper. Bake for 1 hour.

SERVES 4 TO 6

Shepherd's Pie

SHEPHERD'S PIE

2 kg potatoes, peeled and chopped

**1 cup (250 ml) beef or
vegetable stock**

1 bay leaf

2 onions, thinly sliced

3 cloves garlic, thinly sliced

1 kg lean minced topside beef

1 egg white, lightly beaten

**1 tablespoon tomato paste mixed with
1 tablespoon water**

1 tablespoon chopped, fresh parsley

freshly ground black pepper

2 tablespoons white wine

½ cup (125 ml) skim milk

2 tablespoons grated Parmesan cheese

1 Preheat oven to 190°C (375°F).

2 Steam or boil potatoes until tender, then mash and set aside.

3 In a saucepan, bring stock to the boil. Add bay leaf, onions and garlic. Reduce heat, cover and simmer for 5 minutes.

4 Add meat, egg white, tomato paste and water, parsley, pepper and wine. Mix well and simmer for a further 10 minutes. Drain off excess liquid and set aside. Remove bay leaf.

5 Combine potatoes with skim milk and Parmesan cheese. Place meat mixture in large ovenproof dish. Spoon mashed potato over it and bake for 1 hour.

SERVES 4 TO 6

LEEKS WITH CHEESE SAUCE

1 cup (250 ml) water

4 medium-sized leeks, washed, trimmed and sliced in half lengthways

¼ cup finely chopped, fresh parsley, for garnish

CHEESE SAUCE

1 cup ricotta cheese

¾ cup (180 ml) skim milk

2 tablespoons grated Parmesan cheese

freshly ground black pepper

1 In a saucepan bring water to the boil and add leeks. Reduce heat, cover and simmer for 8 minutes. Remove from pan, drain and chill.

2 TO MAKE SAUCE: Blend all the ingredients and chill.

3 Just before serving, pour sauce over leeks and garnish with parsley.

SERVES 4

⅗ HIGHLAND FRUIT SALAD

This is delicious served with low fat yoghurt.

COCK-A-LEEKIE

1½ kg boiling chicken, skinned

12 cups (3 litres) water

1 bay leaf

freshly ground black pepper

1 large white onion, finely chopped

1 kg leeks, trimmed and finely chopped

1 tablespoon finely chopped, fresh parsley

2½ cups (500 g) pitted prunes

1 Place chicken and water in a large saucepan with the bay leaf, pepper, onion and half the leeks. Bring to the boil, cover and simmer for 1½ hours.

2 Strain off soup. Allow chicken to cool, and remove about 2 cups of flesh. Roughly chop.

3 Return stock to pan with remaining leeks, and cook for another 10 minutes. Stir in chicken flesh and chopped parsley.

4 Place several prunes in each bowl and pour in soup. Serve with wholemeal Pritikin bread.

SERVES 4 TO 6

HIGHLAND FRUIT SALAD

1 kg combined fresh strawberries, blackcurrants and raspberries

juice 1 orange

2 tablespoons brandy

dash ground cinnamon

1 Combine all ingredients.

SERVES 4 TO 6

CURRANT SCONES

4 cups raw oats, blended to a fine flour

3 teaspoons baking powder

½ teaspoon mixed spice

¾ cup (125 g) currants, rinsed under cold water and drained well

1 cup (250 ml) skim milk

1 Preheat oven to 220°C (425°F).

2 Combine oat flour with baking powder, mixed spice and currants. Pour in milk and knead lightly to form dough. Roll out to thickness of ½ cm. Use a scone cutter or glass jar, lightly floured, to cut out scone rounds.

3 Place on a non-stick baking tray and brush tops with extra skim milk. Bake for 12 minutes. Wrap cooked scones in clean tea towel until required.

4 Serve with thick fruit purée and low fat yoghurt or Ricotta Whip. If not eaten immediately, reheat in oven for 1 minute before serving.

MAKES 10 TO 12

RICOTTA WHIP

250 g fresh ricotta cheese

¼ cup (60 ml) skim milk

1 teaspoon vanilla essence

1 Blend all ingredients until smooth.

2 Serve as a topping for desserts. Delete vanilla essence and you have an instant creamy base for pasta sauces.

SERVES 4 TO 6

Gifts from Greece

LENTIL SOUP

2½ cups (500 g) yellow lentils, rinsed

1 stalk celery, including 2 to 3 leaves, chopped

1 large onion, chopped

3 bay leaves

2 cloves garlic, chopped

7 cups (1¾ litres) water

freshly ground black pepper

1 tablespoon white vinegar

1 Combine all ingredients except vinegar in a saucepan and bring to the boil. Reduce heat, cover and simmer for 45 minutes.

2 Remove bay leaves, add vinegar and purée soup in blender. Reheat and serve.

SERVES 4 TO 6

❧ GREEK COOKING

Fresh herbs are always preferred. Many dishes are flavoured with dill, parsley, garlic, thyme, mint and sage. Yoghurt, rice and salad are often served as side dishes.

Lentil Soup

EGG AND LEMON SOUP

6 cups (1½ litres) chicken or fish stock

½ cup (90 g) brown rice

3 egg whites, lightly beaten

juice 1 lemon

freshly ground black pepper

1 lemon, thinly sliced, for garnish

1 Bring stock to the boil in a saucepan and add rice. Cover, reduce heat and simmer for 40 minutes.

2 Combine egg whites with lemon juice and 1 cup (250 ml) hot soup. Stir into soup. Heat through, add pepper, garnish with lemon slices and serve.

SERVES 4 TO 6

YOGHURT DIP

1 medium-sized cucumber, peeled and diced

3 cloves garlic, crushed

2 cups (500 ml) low fat yoghurt

2 teaspoons white vinegar

2 teaspoons chopped, fresh mint

freshly ground black pepper

1 Place cucumber in strainer to drain excess liquid.

2 Combine all ingredients, chill and serve.

SERVES 4 TO 6

ZUCCHINI SALAD

1 kg zucchini (courgettes), thinly sliced

juice 1 lemon

juice 2 oranges

1 clove garlic, chopped

1 small white onion, chopped

1 tablespoon chopped, fresh parsley

freshly ground black pepper

1 Combine all ingredients. Chill and serve.

SERVES 4 TO 6

Greek Salad

GREEK SALAD

1 cos lettuce, broken into pieces

2 tomatoes, sliced in wedges

1 small cucumber, sliced

4 radishes, sliced

1 small green capsicum (pepper), sliced

1 small white onion, sliced

125 g fresh ricotta cheese, cut in chunks

DRESSING

1 cup (250 ml) fresh orange juice

1 teaspoon fresh lemon juice

1 teaspoon white vinegar

1 clove garlic, crushed

1 teaspoon dried oregano

freshly ground black pepper

1 Arrange salad ingredients in bowl.

2 Combine dressing ingredients, pour over salad and serve.

SERVES 4 TO 6

Souvlakia

🌰 PINE NUTS

These are an excellent source of B vitamins, iron and protein. They contain no cholesterol.

SOUVLAKIA

1 kg beef or lamb fillets, trimmed of all visible fat and diced

MARINADE

2 tablespoons fresh, chopped oregano or 2 teaspoons dried oregano

3 cloves garlic, finely chopped

juice 2 lemons

1 cup (250 ml) dry white wine

freshly ground black pepper

1 Combine marinade ingredients and marinate beef overnight.

2 Thread on to metal or bamboo skewers. (Pre-soak bamboo skewers overnight in water to prevent burning.)

3 Grill for 10 to 12 minutes, basting regularly with marinade. Serve with salad.

SERVES 4 TO 6

STUFFED TOMATOES

8 medium-sized tomatoes

2 tablespoons pine nuts, lightly toasted

1 large white onion, finely chopped

freshly ground black pepper

1 cup cooked brown rice

2 tablespoons finely chopped, fresh parsley

1 tablespoon finely chopped, fresh mint

1 tablespoon currants

1 cup (250 ml) water

juice 1 lemon

1 Preheat oven to 180°C (350°F).

2 Slice tops off tomatoes and set aside. Scoop out pulp and mix with pine nuts, onion and pepper. Simmer in a saucepan for 5 minutes.

3 Stir in rice, parsley, mint and currants and heat through.

4 Pile mixture into tomato cases and replace sliced-off tops. Put tomatoes in an ovenproof dish. Pour in 1 cup (250 ml) water and lemon juice. Bake for 30 minutes and serve.

SERVES 4 TO 6

MOUSSAKA

1½ kg eggplants (aubergine)

MEAT SAUCE

½ cup (125 ml) water

2 large white onions, finely chopped

3 cloves garlic, chopped

1 kg lean minced topside beef

3 tablespoons tomato paste mixed with ¼ cup (60 ml) water

2 very ripe tomatoes, chopped

¼ cup chopped, fresh parsley

½ cup (125 ml) red or white wine

1 teaspoon cinnamon

freshly ground black pepper

WHITE SAUCE

6 tablespoons wholemeal flour

4 cups (1 litre) skim milk

4 egg whites

2 tablespoons grated Parmesan cheese

dash nutmeg

1 Preheat oven to 180°C (350°F).

2 Cut eggplants into medium-sized slices. Place on kitchen paper for 20 minutes to absorb bitter juices, then rinse and pat dry. Steam until tender and set aside.

3 **TO MAKE MEAT SAUCE:** Bring water to boil in a saucepan and add onions and garlic. Reduce heat, cover and simmer for 5 minutes.

4 Add meat and sauté for a further 5 minutes. Add remaining meat sauce ingredients. Cover and simmer for 20 minutes on low heat. Drain off excess liquid and set aside.

5 **TO MAKE WHITE SAUCE:** Mix flour and milk in a saucepan. Bring to the boil, stirring continuously for 2 minutes. Add egg whites, Parmesan and nutmeg. Cook for a further 2 minutes.

6 Layer a 24 x 30 x 5 cm ovenproof dish alternating with eggplant and meat mixture, finishing with eggplant. Pour over white sauce and bake for 1 hour. Allow to stand for several minutes before cutting.

SERVES 4 TO 5

CHEESE PIE

150 g cottage cheese

2 tablespoons grated Parmesan cheese

1 egg white, lightly beaten

2 tablespoons chopped, fresh parsley

dash nutmeg

freshly ground black pepper

¼ cup (60 ml) skim milk

12 sheets filo pastry

1 Preheat oven to 190°C (375°F).

2 Combine cottage and Parmesan cheeses with egg white, parsley, nutmeg and pepper.

3 Layer a round 20 cm non-stick baking tin with 6 folded sheets of filo. Brush each sheet separately with skim milk.

4 Pour in cheese mixture and press flat. Top with remaining folded layers of pastry. Brush each sheet with milk.

5 Trim overlapping pastry edges with scissors and tuck in firmly. Brush top of pie with extra milk. Bake for 30 minutes. Cut into wedges and serve.

SERVES 4 TO 6

❧ SOYA MILK

As an alternative to milk in any recipe, use soya milk which is 100% cholesterol-free. Make sure you get the low fat one.

🦋 **RICOTTA CHEESE**

Make sure you buy ricotta which is made from skim milk not whole milk, to ensure a low fat content. Buy only in small quantities as it does not keep very well.

PRAWNS WITH RICOTTA CHEESE

125 g fresh ricotta cheese

½ cup (125 ml) water

2 large white onions, chopped

3 cloves garlic, chopped

3 cups chopped very ripe tomatoes

1 tablespoon tomato paste

1 cup (250 ml) white wine

2 tablespoons chopped, fresh parsley

1 teaspoon dried oregano

freshly ground black pepper

1 kg large uncooked green prawns, shelled and deveined, tails left on

chopped parsley, extra, for garnish

1 Dice ricotta cheese and lightly toast under griller. Set aside.

2 Bring water to the boil in a saucepan. Add onions and garlic. Reduce heat and simmer for 3 to 4 minutes.

3 Add tomatoes, tomato paste, white wine, parsley, oregano and pepper. Cover and simmer for 30 minutes.

4 Add prawns and cook for 3 to 4 minutes or until tender.

5 Top with ricotta cheese cubes and garnish with extra chopped parsley.

SERVES 4 TO 6

BAKED FISH WITH GARLIC

1 x 800 g whole fish

8 cloves garlic, crushed

juice 1 lemon

1 tablespoon white vinegar

¼ cup chopped, fresh parsley

1 teaspoon dried marjoram

freshly ground black pepper

1 Preheat oven to 190°C (375°F).

2 Rinse fish, pat dry and place on a sheet of foil.

3 Combine garlic with lemon juice, vinegar, parsley, marjoram and pepper. Pour over fish.

4 Wrap up fish in foil, place in a baking dish and bake for 40 minutes. Serve with salad.

SERVES 4 TO 6

CHICKEN PIE

1½ kg chicken breasts, skinned and roughly chopped

2 large white onions, chopped

2 bay leaves

2 cloves garlic, chopped

2 tablespoons chopped, fresh parsley

freshly ground black pepper

2½ cups (625 ml) water

12 sheets filo pastry

¼ cup (60 ml) skim milk

SAUCE

4 tablespoons wholemeal flour

1½ cups (375 ml) skim milk

2 tablespoons grated Parmesan cheese

4 egg whites, lightly beaten

dash nutmeg

1 Preheat oven to 190°C (375°F).

2 Place chicken, onion, bay leaves, garlic, parsley, pepper and water in a saucepan. Bring to the boil. Reduce heat, cover and simmer for 20 minutes. Drain, remove bay leaves and set aside.

3 TO MAKE SAUCE: Combine flour and milk and bring to the boil, stirring continuously. Reduce heat. Stir in cheese, egg whites and nutmeg.

4 Pour sauce over chicken mixture and allow to cool. Blend for a few seconds only.

5 Line an ovenproof dish with 6 layers of filo pastry. Brush each sheet separately with skim milk. Pour in chicken mixture and top with remaining pastry sheets. Sprinkle with extra skim milk.

6 Trim off overlapping filo pastry with scissors. Tuck in pastry around edges. Bake for 30 minutes.

SERVES 4 TO 6

MIDDLE EASTERN CUISINE

FISH AND CRACKED WHEAT PATTIES

1 cup finely ground burghul (cracked wheat)

500 g fish fillets, skinned

1 medium-sized white onion, chopped

3 cloves garlic, chopped

1 cup chopped, fresh coriander or parsley

½ teaspoon cayenne pepper

freshly ground black pepper

1 egg white, lightly beaten

lemon wedges, for garnish

1 Soak burghul in cold water for 30 minutes. Drain well and press out all water.

2 Blend fish, onion and garlic until smooth. Mix in bowl with chopped coriander, peppers and egg white.

3 Take small amounts of mixture and form into flattish patties. Preheat a non-stick frypan and cook patties until brown (about 8 minutes each side). Garnish with lemon wedges and serve.

SERVES 4 TO 6

✍ FRESH HERBS

Middle Eastern cuisine is very simple to prepare – pile on the fresh herbs, including parsley, dill, mint and garlic.

Fish and Cracked Wheat Patties

FALAFEL

500 g dried chickpeas, soaked overnight and skins discarded

4 cloves garlic

6 spring onions

1 bunch fresh parsley, stalks removed

1 teaspoon cayenne pepper

freshly ground black pepper

1½ teaspoons freshly ground coriander

2 teaspoons freshly ground cumin

4 egg whites, lightly beaten

lemon wedges, for garnish

1 Preheat oven to 200°C (400°F).

2 Grind chickpeas until they resemble fine crumbs.

3 Blend garlic, spring onions and parsley until smooth. Add ground chickpeas to garlic mixture. Combine with peppers, coriander, cumin and 2 egg whites.

4 Take small amounts of mixture, knead well and roll into small balls. Brush with remaining egg whites and place on a non-stick baking tray. Bake for 30 minutes until brown. Serve with tabouli salad, hoummos, lemon wedges and wholemeal pita bread.

SERVES 4 TO 6

HOUMMOS

125 g dried chickpeas, soaked overnight and skins discarded

5 cloves garlic, chopped

½ cup tahini (optional)

juice 3 lemons

1 teaspoon paprika

fresh parsley sprigs, for garnish

1 Boil the soaked chickpeas for 1 hour and drain.

2 Blend with garlic until smooth and set aside. Add tahini to chickpeas and garlic.

3 Stir in lemon juice. Sprinkle with paprika. Garnish with parsley and serve with wholemeal pita bread.

SERVES 4 TO 6

BABA GHANOUSH

2 medium-sized eggplants (aubergine)

4 cloves garlic, finely chopped

¾ cup (100 ml) fresh lemon juice

1 teaspoon ground cumin

freshly ground black pepper

2 tablespoons tahini (optional)

fresh parsley, chopped and tomato wedges, for garnish

1 Preheat griller or oven at 180°C (350°F).

2 Grill or bake eggplants until skin blisters and turns black. Peel eggplants while hot. Roughly chop flesh, purée and set aside.

3 Stir garlic into eggplant purée. Add lemon juice, cumin and pepper.

4 Swirl tahini through purée.

5 Garnish with parsley and tomato wedges and serve with wholemeal crackers or pita bread.

SERVES 4 TO 6

TABOULI SALAD

1 cup finely ground burghul (cracked wheat)

1 large bunch fresh parsley, finely chopped and stalks removed

½ cup finely chopped, fresh mint

1 small white onion, finely diced

juice 3 to 4 lemons

freshly ground black pepper

3 tomatoes, diced and seeds removed

lettuce leaves, for garnish

1 Cover burghul with cold water and soak for 30 minutes. Drain and press out excess water.

2 Mix burghul with all other ingredients except tomatoes. Top with diced tomatoes and serve with lettuce leaves.

SERVES 4 TO 6

LEBANESE LADIES FINGERS

1 cup (250 ml) vegetable or chicken stock

1 medium-sized white onion, finely chopped

1 large bunch spinach, finely chopped and stalks removed

½ teaspoon freshly grated nutmeg

½ teaspoon cinnamon

1 teaspoon finely chopped, fresh dill

freshly ground black pepper

6 sheets filo pastry, cut in half

½ cup (125 ml) skim milk

fresh parsley sprigs and lemon wedges, for garnish

1 Preheat oven to 190°C (375°F).

2 Bring stock to the boil and add onion. Reduce heat, cover and simmer for 5 minutes.

3 Add chopped spinach, cover and simmer for 4 minutes. Remove spinach from pan. Drain off all excess liquid.

4 Add nutmeg, cinnamon, dill and pepper to spinach and mix until well combined. Allow to cool.

5 Take small amount of mixture and place along lower edge of 1 sheet of pastry. Roll up about half-way. Fold in edges like an envelope and neatly roll up completely. Seal edges with dash of skim milk. Repeat process 12 times.

6 Sprinkle rolls with skim milk. Place on a non-stick baking tray and bake for 35 minutes until brown. Garnish with parsley and lemon wedges and serve.

SERVES 4 TO 6

IRANIAN STUFFED CHICKEN

¼ cup (60 ml) water

1 small white onion, chopped

400 g lean minced beef

1½ cups cooked brown rice

½ teaspoon mixed spice

1 tablespoon pine nuts (optional), lightly toasted

2 bay leaves

½ cup (100 g) mixed dried fruit, rinsed under cold water and drained

2 teaspoons finely chopped, fresh parsley

freshly ground black pepper

1½ kg chicken, skinned

¼ cup (60 ml) lemon juice

1 Preheat oven to 200°C (400°F).

2 Bring water to the boil in a non-stick frypan. Add onion, cover and simmer for 5 minutes. Remove from pan.

3 Add beef and sauté for 5 minutes.

4 Combine beef and onion with rice, mixed spice, pine nuts, bay leaves, dried fruit, parsley and pepper and mix thoroughly.

Stuff mixture into cavity of chicken. Truss with skewer and brush with lemon juice. Cover with foil and bake for 40 minutes.

5 Reduce heat to 180°C (350°F). Remove foil and cook for a further 40 minutes until brown. Serve with vegetables or salad.

SERVES 4 TO 6

TABOULI SALAD

The name of this famous dish can be spelt in a variety of ways e.g. tabouleh and tabbouli.

Iranian Stuffed Chicken

EASTERN DELICACIES

Eastern recipes adapt very easily to low cholesterol cooking because traditional dishes are often based on rice, use a sauce made mostly from fruits, vegetables and spices, and add only small quantities of animal protein (meat, fish or chicken) as a delicious garnish.

Thai food is one of the world's hottest cuisines, so if you prefer milder food, use less than the recommended quantity of chillies.

The Japanese are the longest living race on earth. Their diet is naturally healthy but you may wish to cut back further, by reducing salty ingredients such as soy sauce, dried bonito fish flakes, miso paste and dried seaweed.

Indian cuisine varies enormously, and while much of the food is aromatic, the flavours are often mild. Indian food improves with age — the flavours intensify, so don't throw out any leftovers.

Chinese cooking is one of the great cuisines of the world. The Chinese also have a very low incidence of heart disease, attributable to their low fat diet, so Chinese dishes make a wonderful addition to low cholesterol cooking. The main secret is to stir-fry quickly in a non-stick pan or wok, using stock or water, not oil. None of these recipes use monosodium glutamate.

Vietnamese food is a particularly good choice if you are following a low fat diet, because the emphasis is on very light meals. Many dishes are boiled or steamed and always accompanied by side dishes of fresh raw vegetables.

Enjoy all these exotic flavours from the East!

Spicy Sour Prawn Soup, Cucumber Salad and
Grilled Coriander and Garlic Chicken

FIERY FOOD FROM THAILAND

CHICKEN AND MUSHROOM SOUP

3 cloves garlic, finely chopped

1 tablespoon finely chopped, fresh coriander

1 teaspoon freshly ground black pepper

6 cups (1½ litres) chicken stock

500 g uncooked chicken fillets, diced

1 tablespoon fish sauce

125 g button mushrooms, halved

4 spring onions, finely chopped, for garnish

1 Combine garlic, coriander and pepper. Dry-fry in a large saucepan for 1 to 2 minutes.

2 Add all ingredients except spring onions and bring to the boil. Reduce heat and simmer for 10 to 12 minutes.

3 Garnish with spring onions and serve.

SERVES 4 TO 6

CUCUMBER SALAD

1 medium-sized cucumber, peeled, finely diced and seeds removed

1 fresh red chilli, thinly sliced and seeds removed

3 spring onions, thinly sliced

1 tablespoon fresh lemon juice

1 tablespoon salt-reduced soy sauce

2 teaspoons white vinegar

freshly ground black pepper

fresh coriander leaves, chopped, for garnish

1 Combine all ingredients, garnish with coriander leaves and serve.

SERVES 4 TO 6

SPICY SOUR PRAWN SOUP

500 g fresh uncooked (green) prawns

7 cups (1¾ litres) water

2 stalks lemon grass, tender part only, finely chopped

3 Kaffir lime leaves

1 tablespoon fish sauce

4 fresh red or green chillies, thinly sliced and seeds removed

100 g button mushrooms, halved

3 tablespoons fresh lemon or lime juice

GARNISH

1 bunch fresh coriander leaves, roughly chopped

4 spring onions, chopped

1 Shell and devein prawns but leave tails intact. Rinse prawn heads and crush slightly.

2 Bring water to the boil. Add prawn heads, lemon grass, lime leaves, fish sauce and chillies. Boil for 2 minutes then reduce heat and simmer slowly for 10 minutes. Strain through a fine sieve.

3 Add prawns, mushrooms and lemon juice. Bring to the boil then immediately reduce heat and simmer for 3 minutes only.

4 Swirl through coriander and spring onions and serve.

SERVES 4 TO 6

Massaman Vegetable Curry

MASSAMAN VEGETABLE CURRY

12 dried red chillies

1 tablespoon coriander seeds

1 tablespoon cumin seeds

3 cardamom pods

2 whole cloves

½ teaspoon freshly grated nutmeg

1 teaspoon whole peppercorns

1 small stick cinnamon

2 cups (500 ml) water

5 cloves garlic, finely chopped

2 stalks lemon grass, tender part only, finely chopped

2 medium-sized white onions, thinly sliced

500 g potatoes, peeled

500 g mixed vegetables (carrots, cauliflower, pumpkin, broccoli), chopped

2 tablespoons fish sauce

1 tablespoon white vinegar

1 cup (250 ml) low-fat yoghurt

1 Grind first 8 ingredients (spices) until powdered. Dry-fry in a non-stick frypan until they are smoking vigorously. Remove spices and set aside.

2 Bring ½ cup (125 ml) water to the boil in a large saucepan and add garlic, lemon grass and onions. Reduce heat, cover and simmer for 5 minutes. Add ground spices and simmer, stirring, for 1 minute.

3 Combine vegetables, fish sauce and vinegar with remaining 1½ cups (375 ml) water and add to pan. Bring to the boil. Reduce heat, cover and simmer slowly for 40 minutes.

4 Stir in yoghurt and serve with brown rice.

SERVES 4 TO 6

HOT RED BEEF CURRY

This is one of my favourite curries. It is fiery, but delicious!

1 kg topside beef, trimmed of all visible fat and diced

2 cups (500 ml) beef, chicken or vegetable stock

2 teaspoons cornflour

1 tablespoon fish sauce

RED CURRY PASTE

8 fresh red chillies (including seeds)

2 stalks of lemon grass, tender part only

¼ cup chopped, fresh coriander

4 spring onions, chopped

4 cloves garlic

1 tablespoon chopped, fresh ginger root

freshly ground black pepper

1 TO MAKE RED CURRY PASTE: Blend or pound ingredients until well mashed.

2 Preheat non-stick frypan. Sauté beef for 5 minutes and set aside. Pour in ¼ cup (60 ml) stock and bring to the boil.

3 Add curry paste, reduce heat and simmer uncovered for 2 minutes.

4 Mix remaining 1¾ cups (440 ml) stock with cornflour. Add to pan with beef and fish sauce. Cover and simmer slowly for 1 hour until beef is tender.

5 Before serving, reduce excess liquid by simmering uncovered for 10 to 15 minutes. Allow curry to stand for at least 1 hour before serving. (It tastes even better the next day!) Serve with brown rice.

SERVES 4 TO 6

Hot Red Beef Curry

GRILLED FISH WITH CHILLI SAUCE

1 whole fish, rinsed, patted dry and scored on both sides

CHILLI SAUCE

5 fresh red chillies, chopped and seeds removed

1 tablespoon fish sauce

4 cloves garlic, finely chopped

1 tablespoon finely chopped, fresh ginger root

juice 1 orange

juice 1 lime

1 tablespoon chopped, fresh coriander

½ cup (125 ml) water mixed with 2 teaspoons cornflour

1 Preheat griller to high. Cook fish on both sides and set aside. Keep warm.

2 TO MAKE THE CHILLI SAUCE: Blend all sauce ingredients. Stir in water and cornflour mix and bring to the boil. Reduce heat and simmer, stirring, for 3 minutes.

3 Pour sauce over fish. Serve with brown rice.

SERVES 4 TO 6

HOT GREEN FISH CURRY

2 teaspoons ground coriander

2 teaspoons ground cumin

1 teaspoon ground nutmeg

1 teaspoon finely ground pepper

8 fresh green chillies, chopped and seeds removed

4 cloves garlic, chopped

1 stalk lemon grass, tender part only

1 tablespoon chopped, fresh coriander

2 spring onions, chopped

1 teaspoon lemon zest

1 teaspoon fresh lime juice

½ cup (125 ml) water

1 tablespoon dried galangal, chopped

2 teaspoons cornflour

1 kg fish fillets, cut into small chunks

10 uncooked fresh prawns, shelled, deveined and chopped

1 Preheat non-stick frypan and dry-fry coriander, cumin, nutmeg and pepper until they start to smoke. Remove from pan.

2 Purée chillies, garlic, lemon grass, coriander, spring onions, lemon zest and lime juice. Combine this mixture with ground spices and mash into a paste.

3 Bring ¼ cup water (125 ml) to the boil. Add curry paste and galangal. Cover and simmer 2 to 3 minutes.

4 Mix cornflour with remaining water and add to pan, with fish and prawns. Stir until well combined and simmer uncovered for 10 to 12 minutes. Serve with brown rice.

SERVES 4 TO 6

THAI FISH CAKES

500 g uncooked fish fillets, roughly chopped (select fish which has few bones)

3 tablespoons low-fat yoghurt

1 tablespoon fish sauce

100 g fresh green beans, trimmed and chopped

1 stalk lemon grass, tender part chopped

1 tablespoon green capsicum, chopped

1 tablespoon cornflour

2 cloves fresh garlic, chopped

2 to 3 fresh red or green chillies, chopped and seeds removed

2 teaspoons chopped, fresh coriander leaves

1 egg white

1 Place all ingredients in a blender for a few seconds only, or mash to a fine paste. Chill in refrigerator overnight or for at least 2 hours.

2 Form mixture into small, flat fish cakes.

3 Preheat a non-stick frypan to very hot and cook fish cakes for 2 to 3 minutes each side until brown. Serve with a sweet and sour dipping sauce or lemon wedges.

MAKES 18 TO 20 FISH CAKES

❧ GALANGAL

Galangal is an aromatic herb with a gingery-peppery taste. It can be bought in powdered form and stored in an airtight jar. You can buy the fresh root from Asian stores — it will keep in the refrigerator for a week.

❧ THAI FISH CAKES

Traditionally, Thai fish cakes are deep-fried, but these are cooked in a non-stick frypan. They taste the same, but they're not greasy.

SEAFOOD WITH BASIL AND MINT

1 kg mixed seafood (fish fillets, prawns, calamari rings)

1 cup (250 ml) water

1 white onion, roughly chopped

2 cloves garlic, chopped

2 fresh red chillies, chopped and seeds removed

2 stalks lemon grass, tender part only, finely chopped

2 tablespoons fish sauce

1 tablespoon fresh lime juice

½ cup chopped, fresh basil leaves

½ cup chopped, fresh mint leaves

1 tablespoon finely chopped, fresh coriander leaves

1 Chop fish fillets into small chunks. Shell and devein prawns, leaving tails intact. Set aside.

2 Bring water to the boil in large non-stick frypan. Add onion, garlic, chillies and lemon grass. Cover and simmer for 5 minutes.

3 Add the mixed seafood, cover and simmer for 4 to 5 minutes.

4 Combine fish sauce with lime juice, basil, mint and coriander. Lightly stir into frypan, heat through and serve with brown rice.

SERVES 4 TO 6

STEAMED FISH WITH GINGER SAUCE

1 kg fish fillets, or 1 whole fish

fresh coriander leaves, for garnish

GINGER SAUCE

1 tablespoon chopped fresh ginger root

1 teaspoon vinegar

2 tablespoons salt-reduced soy sauce

1 tablespoon fish sauce

2 cloves garlic, chopped

4 spring onions, chopped

1 tablespoon cornflour, mixed with ½ cup (125ml) water

1 tablespoon fresh orange or apple juice

1 Blend together all sauce ingredients and place in a saucepan. Simmer, stirring, until sauce reaches boiling point. Reduce heat, simmer and stir for another minute.

2 Steam fish for about 8 minutes, until flesh is white and flakes. Pour Ginger Sauce over fish.

3 Garnish with coriander and serve.

SERVES 4 TO 6

CHILLI CHICKEN WITH BASIL

1 cup (250 ml) chicken stock

4 cloves garlic, finely chopped

3 fresh red chillies, finely chopped and seeds removed

1 kg chicken pieces, skinned and chopped into bite-sized pieces

1 cup chopped, fresh basil leaves

1 tablespoon fish sauce

juice 1 lemon

1 Bring chicken stock to the boil in a non-stick frypan. Add garlic and chillies and sauté for 1 minute.

2 Add the chicken pieces. Cover and simmer on a low heat for 40 minutes.

3 Stir in the basil leaves and fish sauce. Heat through. Sprinkle with lemon juice and serve.

SERVES 4 TO 6

❧ CORIANDER

Although you can use substitutes for some ingredients, it is worth searching for authentic Thai herbs and spices. Most Asian food stores stock imported and locally produced ingredients. Never substitute parsley for fresh coriander — this gives Thai cuisine its quintessential flavour.

GRILLED CORIANDER AND GARLIC CHICKEN

1 kg chicken pieces, skinned

fresh coriander sprigs, for garnish

MARINADE

12 cloves garlic

2 bunches fresh coriander

2 teaspoons freshly ground pepper

2 fresh red chillies, seeds removed

1 tablespoon fresh lemon juice

1 Blend marinade ingredients and rub over chicken pieces. Refrigerate overnight or for at least 3 hours.

2 Grill or barbecue chicken pieces.

3 Garnish with coriander and serve.

SERVES 4 TO 6

SATAY KEBABS

Traditionally, kebabs are served with peanut sauce, but all nuts except chestnuts are excluded from most low cholesterol menus. Vegetarians can substitute tofu or vegetables for chicken, beef or seafood.

500 g beef fillet or 500 g chicken fillet or 500 g mixed seafood pieces

SATAY MARINADE

4 fresh red or green chillies, chopped and seeds removed

5 cloves garlic, chopped

1 stalk lemon grass, tender part only

1 teaspoon ground turmeric

1 tablespoon fish sauce

2 teaspoons finely chopped, fresh ginger root

juice 1 lime

juice 1 orange

½ cup (125 ml) low fat yoghurt

1 tablespoon finely chopped, fresh coriander

freshly ground black pepper

1 Remove all visible fat from beef or chicken and cut into small chunks.

2 TO MAKE MARINADE: Combine all ingredients and blend.

3 Marinate beef, chicken or seafood in satay marinade in the refrigerator for at least 2 hours.

4 Thread kebabs on to metal or presoaked bamboo skewers.

5 Preheat griller to high and cook kebabs for 2 to 3 minutes each side. Kebabs can also be barbecued.

SERVES 4 TO 6

Satay kebabs served on a bed of lettuce

TASTE OF JAPAN

DASHI

40 g kombu (dried sea kelp)
6 cups (1½ litres) water
½ cup bonito fish flakes

1 Rinse kombu in cold water. Add to water in a saucepan and bring slowly to the boil. Just before water reaches boiling point, remove from heat and discard kombu.

2 Return water to heat and add bonito flakes. Bring to the boil. Immediately remove from heat and let the flakes settle in the bottom of the pan.

3 Strain the dashi through a sieve and use for soups, sautés and sauces.

MAKES 6 CUPS (1½ LITRES)

❧ DASHI

Dashi is a stock used in many Japanese recipes. It is made with dried sea kelp (kombu) and dried bonito fish flakes, available in Asian and some health food stores. Dashi is essential if you want your Japanese recipes to have an authentic flavour.

Tofu and Noodle Soup with Vegetable Tempura

TOFU AND NOODLE SOUP

100 g soba buckweat noodles

½ cup (125 ml) mirin (rice wine)

½ cup (125 ml) salt-reduced soy sauce

300 g fresh tofu, diced

6 cups (1½ litres) dashi (see recipe)

3 spring onions, finely chopped

1 Bring a large saucepan of water to the boil. Plunge in noodles and cook until tender. Drain and set aside.

2 Bring mirin and soy sauce to the boil. Add diced tofu, reduce heat and simmer for 4 minutes.

3 Add noodles and dashi and heat through. Sprinkle with spring onions and serve.

SERVES 4 TO 6

MISO SOUP

2 dried shitake mushrooms

6 cups (1½ litres) dashi (see recipe)

2 tablespoons low-salt miso paste

2 tablespoons grated carrot

3 spring onions, finely chopped

1 Soak mushrooms in hot water for 30 minutes. Drain, trim off stalks and slice.

2 Bring dashi to the boil. Immediately remove from heat.

3 Mix 1 cup (250 ml) of dashi with miso paste. Return to saucepan and add mushrooms and grated carrot. Simmer for 2 minutes. Sprinkle with spring onions and serve.

SERVES 4 TO 6

CHICKEN AND VEGETABLE SOUP

3 dried shitake mushrooms

6 cups (1½ litres) dashi (see recipe)

3 spring onions, finely chopped

1 chicken fillet, thinly sliced

1 stalk celery, finely diced

1 small carrot, cut into thin strips

1 Soak mushrooms in hot water for 30 minutes. Remove from water. Cut off stalks and cut mushrooms into thin slices.

2 Bring dashi to the boil and add all other ingredients. Reduce heat and simmer on a low heat for 8 minutes.

SERVES 4 TO 6

SPINACH SALAD

16 spinach leaves

DRESSING

¼ cup (60 ml) salt-reduced soy sauce

1 tablespoon dried bonito flakes

2 teaspoons sesame seeds, toasted

squeeze fresh lemon juice

1 Remove centre stalk of spinach leaves. Blanch leaves for 1 minute in boiling water. Remove and drain. Chop into pieces.

2 Combine dressing ingredients and pour over spinach. Chill and serve.

SERVES 4 TO 6

SEAWEED SALAD

45 g dried wakame seaweed

chopped spring onions, for garnish

DRESSING

1 tablespoon sesame seeds, toasted

2 tablespoons low-salt miso paste

1 tablespoon rice vinegar

1 Rinse wakame thoroughly under cold water, then soak, covered in warm water, for 15 minutes. Rinse again and drain thoroughly. Chop into short lengths.

2 Combine dressing ingredients and pour over wakame. Garnish with spring onions and serve.

SERVES 4 TO 6

❧ SHITAKE MUSHROOMS

These dark brown mushrooms are a stable ingredient in Japanese cooking. They are available in dried form from Asian food stores.

❧ JAPANESE FOOD

A Japanese meal usually begins with a clear seafood or vegetable soup. During the meal it is common to serve a heartier miso soup. Main course dishes include small pieces of marinated grilled chicken or fish, accompanied by rice and vegetables, and followed by green tea and fresh fruit.

There is a great emphasis on presentation. Japanese food is more than sustenance — it is an art form, so get out your best porcelain, arrange some flowers and enjoy delicious, nutritious Japanese cuisine.

SUSHI RICE

3 cups (450 g) brown rice

4 cups (1 litre) water

3 tablespoons rice vinegar

2 tablespoons apple juice concentrate

1 Thoroughly rinse rice.

2 Bring all ingredients to the boil. Reduce heat, cover and simmer on a low heat for 40 minutes. Allow to cool.

SERVES 4 TO 6

NIGIRI SUSHI

fresh seafood pieces (garfish, ocean perch, squid, salmon, prawns), thinly sliced

sushi rice (see recipe)

fresh parsley and spring onions, for garnish

MARINADE

¼ cup (60 ml) dashi (see recipe)

2 tablespoons mirin (rice wine)

2 teaspoons rice vinegar

1 Marinate seafood slices for 30 minutes.

2 Take small amounts of sushi rice and shape into small oval shapes. Top with marinated seafood pieces and arrange decoratively on a plate or wooden board. Garnish with parsley and spring onions and serve.

SERVES 4 TO 6

TUNA ROLL

3 sheets nori (dried seaweed) cut in half

sushi rice (see recipe)

fresh tuna, sliced into thin strips

salt-reduced soy sauce

1 Place one half-sheet nori on a bamboo sushi mat. Spread first half of nori sheet with thin layer of rice.

2 Top with tuna strips and a few drops of soy sauce. Roll up tightly and cut into short lengths. Repeat with remaining nori sheets.

SERVES 4 TO 6

CUCUMBER ROLL

3 sheets nori (dried seaweed) cut in half

sushi rice (see recipe)

½ cucumber, cut into thin strips and seeds removed

salt-reduced soy sauce

1 Place one half-sheet nori on a bamboo sushi mat. Spread small amount of rice over first half of nori sheet.

2 Top with cucumber strips, and sprinkle with a few drops of salt-reduced soy sauce. Carefully roll up tightly. Cut roll into short lengths. Repeat with remaining nori sheets.

3 Serve with soy sauce, for dipping.

SERVES 4 TO 6

VEGETABLE TEMPURA

500 g mixed vegetables (pumpkin, leeks, broccoli, eggplant, capsicum, carrot), all thinly sliced but broccoli broken into florets

lemon wedges, for garnish

BATTER

1 egg white

1 cup (250 ml) iced water

1 cup (125 g) wholemeal flour

¼ teaspoon baking powder

1 Preheat oven to 200°C (400°F).

2 Mix batter ingredients. Dip in vegetable pieces and place on non-stick baking tray. Bake for 15 to 20 minutes until brown. Garnish with lemon wedges and serve with a dipping sauce of salt-reduced soy.

SERVES 4 TO 6

Nigiri Sushi and Cucumber Roll

❧ MIRIN

Mirin is a Japanese rice wine, available at Japanese and some Asian food stores. If unavailable, substitute sherry, but the flavour will be different.

CHICKEN TONKATSU

4 chicken breasts, trimmed of all visible fat and halved

½ cup (125 ml) salt-reduced soy sauce

1 tablespoon mirin (rice wine)

freshly ground black pepper

1 cup (125 g) wholemeal flour

2 egg whites, lightly beaten

1 cup homemade Pritikin breadcrumbs

lemon wedges, for garnish

extra salt-reduced soy sauce, for dipping

1 Marinate chicken breasts in soy sauce, mirin and pepper for 1 hour.

2 Drain, and dip in flour and egg white. Roll in breadcrumbs, pressing firmly. Chill in refrigerator for 30 minutes or in freezer for 10 minutes.

3 Preheat oven to 190°C (375°F).

4 Bake for 30 minutes. Slice into thick strips, garnish with lemon wedges and serve with soy sauce for dipping.

SERVES 4 TO 6

Chicken Tonkatsu

CHICKEN YAKITORI

600 g chicken fillets, trimmed of all visible fat

½ cup (125 ml) salt-reduced soy sauce

½ cup (125 ml) mirin (rice wine)

squeeze fresh lemon juice

1 teaspoon finely grated, fresh ginger root

1 Cut the chicken into small pieces and thread on to metal or presoaked bamboo skewers.

2 Mix together soy sauce, mirin, lemon juice and ginger. Place in a small saucepan and bring to the boil. Immediately remove from the heat and allow to cool.

3 Leave chicken in this marinade for 30 minutes.

4 Preheat griller to high.

5 Cook chicken on both sides for several minutes until tender. Baste during cooking. Serve with brown rice.

SERVES 4 TO 6

PRAWN TEMPURA

1 kg fresh uncooked (green) large prawns, shelled and deveined, tails left on

BATTER

2 egg whites

2 cups (500 ml) iced water

2 cups (500 g) wholemeal flour

½ teaspoon baking powder

TO SERVE

salt-reduced soy sauce

lemon wedges

1 Mix batter ingredients.

2 Dip in prawns and place on a non-stick baking tray. Bake for 15 to 20 minutes until brown.

3 Serve with dipping sauce of salt-reduced soy sauce and lemon wedges.

SERVES 4 TO 6

GRILLED GARFISH

6 medium-sized garfish

½ cup (125 ml) mirin (rice wine)

2 tablespoons salt-reduced soy sauce

1 teaspoon finely grated, fresh ginger root

1 Marinate garfish in mirin, soy sauce and ginger for 30 minutes.

2 Preheat griller to high and cook for 15 minutes.

3 Garnish with lemon wedges and cucumber slices.

SERVES 6

COLD NOODLES WITH NORI

1 cup (250 ml) dashi (see recipe page 48)

¼ cup (60 ml) salt-reduced soy sauce

1 tablespoon grated, fresh ginger root

½ cup (125 ml) mirin (rice wine)

1 tablespoon bonito flakes

200 g soba buckweat noodles

3 sheets nori (dried seaweed)

4 spring onions, finely chopped

1 Combine dashi, soy sauce, ginger, mirin and bonito flakes. Bring almost to the boil and strain through a sieve. Allow to cool.

2 Bring a large saucepan of water to the boil and add noodles. Cook until tender. Drain and rinse under cold running water. Place noodles in individual serving bowls with 1 to 2 ice cubes in each.

3 Toast nori under griller. Crumble toasted nori over the noodles.

4 Pour sauce over noodles. Garnish with spring onions and serve.

SERVES 4 TO 6

Flavours vary enormously and can be aromatic or spicy. India is a vegetarian's delight. Meat, fish and chicken are eaten in small quantities, with meals being based on rice, vegetables and legumes, bread and milk products.

AROMATIC DISHES FROM INDIA

WHOLEMEAL CHAPATIS

2½ cups (560 g) wholemeal flour

1 cup (250 ml) water

1 tablespoon skim milk

1 Sift flour and gradually add water and milk. Combine well and knead for 10 minutes on a lightly floured board. Wrap in plastic wrap or slightly damp cloth and allow to stand for 2 hours.

2 Form small pieces of dough into balls and roll out as thin as a crêpe.

3 Preheat a non-stick frypan. Cook chapatis for 1 minute. Press edges with a cloth to make the chapatis light and bubbly. Turn over and cook for another minute.

4 Wrap cooked chapatis in clean tea towel and serve with curries and chutney.

SERVES 4 TO 6

PAKORAS

800 g mixed vegetables (broccoli, cauliflower, capsicum, eggplant, onions, potato, pumpkin), chopped into bitesize pieces

BATTER

2 cups (500 g) wholemeal or besan (chickpea) flour

½ teaspoon baking powder

2 cups (500 ml) water

2 egg whites, lightly beaten

½ teaspoon ground turmeric

1 teaspoon cumin seeds

freshly ground black pepper

1 Preheat oven to 190°C (375°F).

2 **TO MAKE BATTER:** Sift flour and baking powder. Add water and combine well. Add all other batter ingredients.

3 Dip in vegetable pieces and place on a non-stick baking tray. Bake for 25 minutes until brown. Serve with low fat yoghurt or chutney dip.

SERVES 4 TO 6

VEGETABLE SAMOSAS

DOUGH

1½ cups (185 g) wholemeal flour

pinch baking powder

½ cup (125 ml) water

1½ tablespoons skim milk

SAMOSA FILLING

3 to 4 potatoes (about 800 g), peeled and chopped

¾ cup (185 ml) water

1 large onion, thinly sliced

2 cloves garlic, finely chopped

1 cup fresh or frozen peas

1 small carrot, grated

1 teaspoon finely chopped, fresh ginger root

1 teaspoon ground cumin

½ teaspoon ground coriander

½ teaspoon ground turmeric

freshly ground black pepper

1 fresh green chilli, finely chopped or blended with seeds removed

½ cup finely chopped, fresh coriander

2 tablespoons fresh lemon juice

lemon wedges and chutney, for garnish

1 **TO MAKE DOUGH:** Sift flour and baking powder. Add water and milk, combine and knead for 10 minutes. Wrap in plastic and set aside.

2 **TO MAKE FILLING:** Steam or boil the potatoes, and mash.

3 Bring water to the boil. Add onion and garlic. Reduce heat, cover and simmer for 5 minutes.

4 Add peas, carrot and ginger. Cover and simmer for 5 minutes. Drain well. Combine with mashed potato and mix thoroughly.

5 Preheat a non-stick frypan and dry-fry cumin, ground coriander, turmeric and

Vegetable Samosas

pepper until they smoke. Add to filling mixture with chilli, fresh coriander and lemon juice. Mix well and allow to cool.

6 Preheat oven to 190°C (375°F).

7 Take small amounts of dough and form into balls. Roll these out into very thin circles. Cut circles in half. Place 1½ teaspoons of filling on one side of half circle. Fold over to form a triangular shape. Seal edges and brush top with extra skim milk.

8 Bake for 25 minutes until brown. Garnish with lemon wedges and chutney and serve.

(Instead of cutting circles of dough in half, you can form pastie shapes. For a crowd, I sometimes make one large pastie and serve the samosas in thick strips. If there is any samosa mixture over, form into balls, brush with egg white and bake in the oven — easy Indian rissoles!)

SERVES 4 TO 6

CAULIFLOWER WITH YOGHURT

1 small cauliflower, broken into florets

½ teaspoon ground turmeric

freshly ground black pepper

2 teaspoons mustard seeds

1½ cups (375 ml) low fat yoghurt

1 teaspoon finely chopped, fresh ginger root

2 cloves garlic, finely chopped

½ fresh red or green chilli, finely chopped and seeds removed

1 Steam or boil cauliflower until tender. Drain and set aside.

2 Preheat non-stick frypan and dry-fry turmeric, pepper and mustard seeds. When seeds begin to pop, add to yoghurt. Stir in ginger, garlic and chilli.

3 Add cauliflower florets and mix well. Refrigerate for 1 hour and serve.

SERVES 4 TO 6

❧ INDIAN SPICES

Authentic Indian cooks grind their own fresh spices, regarding commercially prepared curry powder with disdain. You can make up your own curry powders by grinding spices quickly and easily in a coffee grinder. Dry-fry them in a preheated non-stick frying pan before adding them to the cooking pot.

PUNJAB POTATO PURÉE

1 kg potatoes, chopped

1 teaspoon ground cumin

1 tablespoon black mustard seeds

1 teaspoon ground coriander

freshly ground black pepper

½ cup (125 ml) water

1 onion, finely chopped

1 clove garlic, finely chopped

1 teaspoon finely chopped, fresh ginger root

¼ cup (60 ml) low fat yoghurt

1 fresh red or green chilli, finely chopped and seeds removed

½ cup finely chopped, fresh coriander

lemon wedges

fresh coriander, chopped

1 Steam or boil potatoes until tender, and reserve.

2 Preheat a non-stick frypan. Dry-fry cumin, mustard seeds, coriander and pepper until smoking and mustard seeds pop, set aside.

3 Bring water to the boil. Add onion, garlic and ginger. Reduce heat, cover and simmer for 5 minutes. Drain and combine with dry-fried spices.

4 Mash potatoes with yoghurt and add in all other ingredients.

5 Garnish with lemon wedges and fresh coriander.

SERVES 4 TO 6

PEAS AND BEANS IN SPICY TOMATO SAUCE

1 onion, chopped

1 clove garlic, chopped

1 teaspoon grated, fresh ginger root

1 fresh red chilli, chopped and seeds removed

¼ cup (60 ml) water

1 heaped teaspoon cumin seeds

1 teaspoon ground turmeric

freshly ground black pepper

3 very ripe tomatoes

2 tablespoons lemon juice

250 g fresh shelled peas

500 g snake or French beans, cut into short lengths

1 Purée onion, garlic, ginger and chilli.

2 Add purée to a pan of boiling water. Cover, reduce heat and simmer 5 minutes.

3 Dry-fry cumin, turmeric and pepper. Add to pan and cook for a further minute.

4 Purée tomatoes and lemon juice and add to pan with peas and beans. Cover and simmer for 5 to 6 minutes and serve.

SERVES 4 TO 6

AVIYAL MIXED VEGETABLES

2 fresh green chillies, seeds removed

1 onion, chopped

1 teaspoon grated, fresh ginger root

2 cloves garlic, chopped

1 cup (250 ml) water

1 teaspoon cumin seeds

2 teaspoons black mustard seeds

½ teaspoon ground turmeric

freshly ground black pepper

1 kg mixed vegetables (potatoes, carrots, beans, capsicum, broccoli, cauliflower), roughly chopped

1 cup (250 ml) low fat yoghurt

½ cup finely chopped, fresh coriander

lemon wedges, for garnish

1 Purée chillies, onion, ginger and garlic.

2 In a casserole, bring water to the boil and add puréed mixture. Cover, reduce heat and simmer for 5 minutes.

3 In a pan, dry-fry cumin and black mustard seeds, turmeric and pepper until seeds pop. Add to casserole, cover and simmer for a further 2 minutes.

4 Add potatoes only, cover and simmer for 15 minutes. Then add other vegetables, cover and simmer for 8 to 10 minutes.

5 Stir in yoghurt and coriander. Garnish with lemon wedges and serve.

SERVES 4 TO 6

BRAISED CABBAGE WITH CUMIN

1¼ cups (310 ml) water

1 large onion, thinly sliced

2 teaspoons finely chopped, fresh ginger root

2 cloves garlic, finely chopped

½ cabbage, finely shredded

2 fresh green chillies, finely chopped and seeds removed

1 teaspoon ground turmeric

2 teaspoons cumin seeds

¼ cup (60 ml) fresh lemon juice

1 Bring water to the boil. Add onion, ginger and garlic. Reduce heat, cover and simmer for 5 minutes.

2 Add cabbage, chillies and turmeric and mix well. Cover, simmer for 15 to 20 minutes.

3 Dry-fry cumin seeds until they smoke. Sprinkle over cabbage. Pour lemon juice over cabbage and serve.

SERVES 4 TO 6

DHAL

2½ cups (500 g) red lentils

6 cups (1½ litres) water

5 cloves garlic, finely chopped

2½ cm piece cinnamon stick

6 black peppercorns

8 cardamom pods, slightly bruised

2 teaspoons ground turmeric

3 teaspoons cumin seeds

1 Wash lentils in colander. Discard any that float to the surface.

2 Place lentils in a heavy-based saucepan with water and all ingredients except cumin seeds. Bring to the boil. Reduce heat, cover and simmer for 45 to 60 minutes. Stir at regular intervals. Add more water if you prefer a thinner dhal.

3 Remove cardamom pods, peppercorns and cinnamon stick. For a smoother texture, blend or mash lentils.

4 Just before serving, heat a non-stick frypan and dry-fry cumin seeds until they start to smoke. Sprinkle heated cumin seeds over dhal.

SERVES 4 TO 6

TAJ MAHAL CHICKEN

1¼ cups (310 ml) chicken stock

2 large white onions, thinly sliced

2 fresh red or green chillies, finely chopped and seeds removed

4 cloves garlic, finely chopped

1 tablespoon finely chopped, fresh ginger root

1½ kg chicken pieces, skinned

1 cup (250 ml) low fat yoghurt

1 cup finely chopped, fresh coriander

2 tablespoons finely chopped, fresh mint leaves

SPICES

2 cardamom pods

2 teaspoons ground turmeric

1 bay leaf

1 teaspoon black mustard seeds

1 teaspoon cumin seeds

1 small piece cinnamon stick

1 clove

3 peppercorns

1 Preheat a non-stick frypan. Add spices and dry-fry. Remove from heat when spices smoke.

2 Bring 1 cup (250 ml) stock to the boil and add onions. Reduce heat, cover and simmer for 4 minutes. Add chillies, garlic and ginger and cook for a further 2 minutes.

3 Stir in dry-fried spices until well combined. Remove this spicy mixture from frypan.

4 Add chicken pieces to frypan and sauté until lightly browned all over. Combine all ingredients except coriander and mint. Cover and simmer on a low heat for 40 minutes. Stir in coriander and mint and serve with brown rice.

SERVES 4 TO 6

🫖 **DHAL**

Serve this with curries and brown rice. Or simply serve with mountains of chapatis for a nutritious and filling meal.

Tandoori Chicken served with salad and Wholemeal Chapatis

TANDOORI CHICKEN

1½ kg chicken pieces, on the bone

1 tablespoon white vinegar

1 cup (250 ml) low fat yoghurt

lemon wedges, for garnish

TANDOORI PASTE

3 fresh red chillies, seeds removed

1 onion, chopped

6 cloves garlic, chopped

1 tablespoon chopped, fresh ginger root

2 tablespoons fresh lemon juice

1 teaspoon ground cumin

1 teaspoon freshly ground black pepper

2 teaspoons ground coriander

2 whole cloves

small piece cinnamon stick

1 bay leaf

dash turmeric

dash nutmeg

1 teaspoon paprika

1 Remove all skin from chicken and prick pieces with a fork.

2 **TO MAKE TANDOORI PASTE:** Purée chillies, onion, garlic, ginger and lemon juice. Place in a bowl.

3 Preheat a non-stick frypan and dry-fry remaining tandoori paste spices until smoking vigorously. Combine with the purée and mix to form a paste.

4 Rub this paste thoroughly into chicken pieces. Sprinkle with vinegar and pour yoghurt on top. Combine well and marinate in refrigerator for at least 24 hours. Stir mixture occasionally.

5 Preheat oven to 190°C (375°F).

6 Place chicken pieces on a rack on a roasting pan. Bake for 35 to 40 minutes until tender. Baste during cooking process with any remaining marinade.

SERVES 4 TO 6

CHILLI CHUTNEY

2 large very ripe tomatoes

4 to 6 cloves garlic

3 x 2½ cm pieces fresh ginger root

1 fresh red chilli, seeds removed

1 small white onion

freshly ground black pepper

fresh mint, for garnish

1 Roughly chop tomatoes, garlic, ginger, chilli and onion, and blend with pepper in food processor.

2 Serve garnished with fresh mint.

SERVES 4 TO 6

KITCHERI

2 cups (300 g) brown rice

2 cups (400 g) red lentils

5 cups (1¼ litres) water

1 large onion, sliced

2 cloves garlic, finely chopped

1 teaspoon finely chopped, fresh
ginger root

2 cardamom pods, slightly bruised

small piece cinnamon stick

1 whole clove

½ teaspoon ground turmeric

1 teaspoon cumin seeds

1 fresh red or green chilli, finely
chopped and seeds removed

1 Rinse rice and lentils, drain and set aside.

2 Bring 1 cup (250 ml) water to the boil
and add onion, garlic and ginger. Reduce
heat, cover and simmer for 5 minutes.

3 Add rice and lentils to the pan and
set aside.

4 In a non-stick frypan, dry-fry cardamom
pods, cinnamon stick, clove, turmeric and
cumin seeds. Remove when smoking.
Reserve the cumin seeds.

5 Add remaining spices and chilli to rice
and lentil mixture.

6 Pour in remaining 4 cups (1 litre) water
and bring to the boil. Reduce heat, cover
and simmer for 45 minutes.

7 Sprinkle with cumin seeds and serve.

SERVES 4 TO 6

KITCHERI

*Kitcheri is a delicious
accompaniment Beef
Koftas (recipe page 61).
Kitcheri should also be
served with
accompaniments such as
chutney, low fat yoghurt
and fresh fruit.*

Kitcheri and Beef Koftas

TANDOORI CHICKEN

*This is one of India's
most celebrated dishes.
This recipe can be used
for meat or seafood, and
I strongly recommend you
use freshly ground spices
to create a genuine
tandoori paste.
Traditionally, Tandoori
Chicken is cooked in a
tandoor, or clay oven,
which gives the chicken a
very special, slightly
smokey flavour. However,
you can produce a
delicious result roasting
in the oven, on the
barbecue, or by grilling.
Serve this dish with fresh
salad and homemade
wholemeal chapatis.*

BEEF KOFTAS

2 fresh red chillies

2 fresh green chillies

3 cloves garlic

1 kg lean minced topside beef

freshly ground black pepper

2 egg whites, lightly beaten

1 tablespoon wholemeal flour

1 tablespoon white vinegar

½ cup chopped, fresh coriander

CURRY SAUCE

¾ cup (185 ml) water

2 onions, finely chopped

1 tablespoon finely chopped, fresh ginger root

½ teaspoon ground turmeric

2 teaspoons freshly ground coriander

1 teaspoon ground cumin

½ cup (125 ml) low fat yoghurt

1 Purée chillies and garlic.

2 Mix together beef, chillies, garlic, pepper and egg whites. Form into small balls, sprinkle with flour and set aside.

3 TO MAKE CURRY SAUCE: Bring ½ cup (125 ml) water to the boil. Add onions and ginger. Reduce heat, cover and simmer for 5 minutes. Set aside.

4 Dry-fry turmeric, coriander and cumin until smoking. Add to onion and ginger mixture with yoghurt and remaining ¼ cup (125 ml) water.

5 Add meatballs, cover and simmer on low heat for 35 to 40 minutes.

6 Add vinegar and chopped fresh coriander and combine well. Heat through and serve. This recipe is ideal served with Kitcheri (recipe page 59).

SERVES 4 TO 6

HOT BEEF VINDALOO

1½ kg topside beef, trimmed of all visible fat and diced

1 cup (250 ml) chicken stock or water

4 medium-sized white onions, thinly sliced

3 fresh red or green chillies, finely chopped and seeds removed

5 cloves garlic, finely chopped

1 tablespoon finely chopped, fresh ginger root

CURRY PASTE

1 teaspoon ground turmeric

1 tablespoon ground coriander

1 teaspoon ground peppercorns

1 teaspoon ground cumin

1 teaspoon ground fenugreek

3 tablespoons brown vinegar

1 tablespoon tomato paste

1 TO MAKE CURRY PASTE: Preheat a non-stick frypan and add ground spices. Heat through; remove from heat when they are smoking. Mix with vinegar and tomato paste until smooth.

2 Pour over meat and marinate for at least 1 hour.

3 Bring ½ cup (125 ml) stock to the boil and add onions. Reduce heat, cover and simmer for 5 minutes.

4 Add chillies, garlic and ginger and cook a further 3 minutes. Remove from frypan and set aside.

5 Add marinated meat and sauté for 10 minutes. Add remaining stock. Cover and simmer on a low heat for 1 hour, until meat is tender. Serve with brown rice.

SERVES 4 TO 6

Hot Beef Vindaloo served with rice and Wholemeal Chapatis

Rajasthani Rice

FAVOURITE FISH CURRY

1 teaspoon ground turmeric

1 tablespoon ground coriander

2 teaspoons ground cumin seeds

freshly ground black pepper

1½ cups (375 ml) water

2 large white onions, thinly sliced

4 cloves garlic, finely chopped

**2 teaspoons finely chopped, fresh
ginger root**

**2 fresh red or green chillies, chopped
and seeds removed**

2 large very ripe tomatoes, roughly chopped

1 teaspoon tomato paste

1 kg firm fish fillets, chopped into thick slices

½ cup chopped, fresh coriander

lemon wedges, for garnish

❧ FISH CURRY

*Before eating this curry,
squeeze a little lemon
juice over it. Serve with
brown rice and
accompaniments.*

1 Preheat a non-stick frypan. Dry-fry turmeric, coriander, cumin and pepper until they are heated through and smoking. Remove from heat and set aside.

2 Pour 1 cup (250 ml) water into pan. Bring to the boil and add onions, garlic, ginger and chillies. Reduce heat, cover and simmer for 5 minutes. Add the spices, tomato pieces and tomato paste. Stir until well combined, then cover and simmer for a further 3 minutes.

3 Add fish pieces and remaining ½ cup (125 ml) water. Gently stir until combined. Cover and simmer on a low heat for 10 to 12 minutes.

4 Before serving, stir in chopped coriander. Garnish with lemon wedges.

SERVES 4 TO 6

RAJASTHANI RICE

3 cardamom pods, slightly bruised

1 small piece cinnamon stick

3 whole cloves

6 black peppercorns

3 cups (450 g) brown rice, well rinsed and drained

1 teaspoon grated orange zest

1 teaspoon grated lemon zest

3 cups (750 ml) water

1 cup (250 ml) fresh orange juice

½ cup (90 g) mixed dried fruit, rinsed under cold water and drained

1 Preheat a non-stick frypan and dry-fry cardamom, cinnamon, cloves and peppercorns until they begin to smoke. Add to rice with all ingredients except dried fruit.

2 Stir until well combined and bring to the boil. Reduce heat, cover and simmer slowly until cooked — about 40 minutes.

3 Mix through dried fruit and serve with curry and accompaniments.

SERVES 4 TO 6

RAITA

1 cucumber, peeled and thinly sliced

1 cup (250 ml) low fat yoghurt

1 clove garlic, minced

pinch chilli powder

freshly ground black pepper

1 Combine all ingredients, chill and serve as a side dish for curries.

SERVES 4 TO 6

BANANAS WITH LEMON

4 bananas, sliced

juice 1 lemon

2 teaspoons grated lemon zest

1 Combine all ingredients, chill and serve as a side dish for curries.

SERVES 4 TO 6

CARDAMOM FRUIT SALAD

1 cup chopped bananas

1 cup chopped peaches

1 cup grapes

1 cup chopped mangoes

1 cup chopped kiwi fruit

8 cardamom pods, seeds finely ground

1 cup (250 ml) low fat yoghurt

3 tablespoons apple juice concentrate

fresh mint sprigs, for garnish

1 Combine all ingredients. Refrigerate for at least 2 hours or overnight.

2 Garnish with mint and serve.

SERVES 4 TO 6

LASSI

A perfect refreshing drink to serve with spicy food.

1 cup (250 ml) low fat yoghurt

2 cups (500 ml) iced water

2 tablespoons apple juice concentrate

few drops rose essence

3 to 4 ice cubes

1 Blend all ingredients and serve.

SERVES 4 TO 6

❧ SIDE DISHES

Bananas with Lemon and Raita are excellent dishes to accompany a hot curry. They are very effective at cooling the palate.

The joy of this dish is that any fresh ingredients can be used. This list of ingredients should serve only as an outline. Vegetarians can use any seasonal vegetables. This traditional steamboat recipe is usually cooked at the table in a charcoal-heated firepot. If a firepot is unavailable, a heatproof bowl and gas burner, or electric frypan, can be used.

CHINESE CUISINE

MONGOLIAN HOT POT

100 g cellophane (bean thread) noodles

8 cups (2 litres) chicken stock

300 g firm fish fillets, cut into bite-sized pieces

300 g beef fillet, thinly sliced

300 g chicken breasts, skinned and thinly sliced

400 g spinach, trimmed and roughly chopped

400 g Chinese cabbage, roughly chopped

400 g fresh tofu

1 Soak cellophane noodles in hot water for 20 minutes. Drain and cut into short lengths.
2 Bring stock to the boil on the stove and transfer 6 cups (1½ litres) of it to the firepot. Keep it at boiling point by placing hot coals in the base of the firepot.
3 Each person cooks his or her own portion of fish, meat or chicken, using either a wire spoon or chopsticks. Various sauces — soy, chilli, ginger, soy/mustard — should be placed in small containers in front of each person. Dip food into sauces before eating.
4 When all the meat has been devoured put vegetables, noodles and tofu into the simmering rich stock. Add remaining stock. Cover and simmer for 10 minutes. Then enjoy the delectable flavours of this amazing soup to round off your Mongolian Hot Pot/steamboat meal.

SERVES 4 TO 6

BASIC STOCKS

To make basic Chinese beef, fish or vegetable stock, replace the chicken in the Basic Chinese Chicken Stock recipe with 3 cups chopped beef, fish or mixed vegetables. Freeze stock for later use.

BASIC CHINESE CHICKEN STOCK

1 chicken, skinned

2 cloves garlic, chopped

1 tablespoon chopped, fresh ginger root

1 medium-sized white onion, roughly chopped

1 carrot, roughly chopped

2 stalks celery, roughly chopped

4 stalks coriander

freshly ground black pepper

6 cups (1½ litres) water

1 Cover all ingredients with the water and bring to the boil. Cover and simmer very slowly for 1½ hours to produce a concentrated flavour.
2 Pour soup through a sieve and place liquid in the refrigerator. Later, skim off fatty surface and strain to eliminate all traces of fat.

SERVES 4 TO 6

GINGER TURNIP SOUP

6 cups (1½ litres) basic Chinese chicken stock (see recipe)

3 cups finely chopped turnips

2 cloves garlic, chopped

1 fresh red or green chilli, finely chopped and seeds removed

1 tablespoon finely chopped, fresh ginger root

3 tablespoons cornflour mixed with 4 tablespoons cold water

3 egg whites, lightly beaten

freshly ground black pepper

½ cup spring onions chopped

1 Bring stock to the boil and add turnips, garlic, chilli and ginger. Cover, simmer for 30 minutes. Purée, and return to saucepan.
2 Add cornflour mixture, egg whites and pepper. Simmer and stir for a further 3 to 4 minutes.
Garnish with spring onions and serve.

SERVES 4 TO 6

A selection of fresh vegetables and meats for Mongolian Hot Pot

CHICKEN AND SWEET CORN SOUP

4 cups fresh corn niblets

6 cups (1½ litres) basic Chinese chicken stock (see recipe page 64)

300 g skinned, shredded chicken

1 medium-sized white onion, chopped

1 clove garlic, finely chopped

1 teaspoon finely chopped, fresh ginger root

freshly ground black pepper

3 heaped tablespoons cornflour mixed with 3 tablespoons cold water

3 egg whites

3 spring onions, chopped

salt-reduced soy sauce

1 Shred 2 cups corn niblets in blender.

2 Bring stock to the boil and add chicken, onion, garlic, ginger and pepper. Reduce heat, simmer for 8 minutes. Add cornflour. Simmer and stir for a further 4 minutes.

3 Swirl through egg whites. Garnish with spring onions and serve with a small amount of soy sauce.

SERVES 4 TO 6

CHICKEN AND MUSHROOM SOUP

5 dried Chinese mushrooms

6 cups (1½ litres) basic Chinese chicken stock (see recipe page 64)

300 g skinned chicken breasts, shredded

1 tablespoon finely chopped, fresh ginger root

2 spring onions, sliced

2 egg whites, lightly beaten

2 large lettuce leaves

1 Soak Chinese mushrooms in hot water for 30 minutes. Discard stems and slice finely.

2 Bring stock to the boil. Add chicken, mushrooms, ginger and spring onions. Bring to the boil again, reduce heat and simmer for 5 minutes. Remove from heat and whisk egg whites through soup.

3 Tear lettuce leaves and place in bottom of individual soup bowls. Ladle hot soup into bowls and serve.

SERVES 4 TO 6

Chicken and Sweet Corn Soup

HOT AND SOUR SOUP

6 dried Chinese mushrooms, soaked in hot water for 30 minutes

1 tablespoon cloud ears (type of mushroom)

5 cups (1¼ litres) basic Chinese chicken stock (see recipe page 64)

1 fresh red chilli, chopped and seeds removed

200 g skinned chicken, shredded

1 tablespoon finely chopped, fresh ginger root

1 cup fresh bean curd (tofu), diced

1 tablespoon salt-reduced soy sauce

1 tablespoon Chinese wine or dry sherry

2 tablespoons white vinegar

1 tablespoon cornflour mixed with 1 tablespoon of cold water

3 egg whites, lightly beaten

freshly ground black pepper

2 spring onions, sliced

1 After soaking mushrooms, discard stems and slice.

2 Soak cloud ears in hot water for 10 minutes. Discard tough bits.

3 Bring stock to the boil. Add Chinese mushrooms, chilli, chicken and ginger. Reduce heat, cover and simmer for 5 minutes.

4 Add bean curd, cloud ears, soy sauce, wine and vinegar. Simmer for 2 minutes. Pour cornflour mixture into soup and bring to the boil for 1 minute.

5 Remove from heat and swirl through egg whites. Season with pepper, and garnish with spring onions.

SERVES 4 TO 6

CUCUMBER IN BLACK BEAN SAUCE

3 cloves garlic, finely chopped

1 tablespoon black soya beans, soaked in cold water for 15 minutes, drained and mashed

1 red chilli, finely chopped and seeds removed

1 spring onion, finely chopped

5 tablespoons basic Chinese vegetable stock (see recipe page 64)

2 medium-sized cucumbers, peeled and sliced

2 tablespoons Chinese wine or dry sherry

1 teaspoon cornflour

freshly ground black pepper

1 Place garlic, black beans, chilli and spring onion in a non-stick frypan. Stir-fry for 2 minutes with 3 tablespoons of stock.

2 Add cucumbers to frypan and stir-fry for 3 minutes.

3 Combine wine, cornflour and remaining stock. Add to frypan and simmer for 1 minute. Season with pepper and serve.

SERVES 4 TO 6

SZECHUAN STEAMED EGGPLANT

1 large eggplant, sliced into discs

SAUCE

4 cloves garlic, finely chopped

3 tablespoons basic Chinese vegetable stock (see recipe page 64)

1 fresh red chilli, finely chopped and seeds removed

1 teaspoon cornflour

2 teaspoons salt-reduced soy sauce

1 tablespoon Chinese wine or dry sherry

freshly ground black pepper

1 Place eggplant slices on kitchen paper for 20 minutes to absorb bitter juices. Rinse and pat dry. Place prepared eggplant slices in a heatproof bowl and steam vigorously for 15 minutes.

2 **TO MAKE SAUCE:** Stir-fry garlic in 1 tablespoon stock. Combine remaining sauce ingredients and add to wok or frying pan. Cover and simmer for 2 minutes.

3 Remove eggplant from steamer. Drain, spoon sauce over and serve.

SERVES 4 TO 6

Spring Rolls with a Dipping Sauce

SPRING ROLLS

For a vegetarian meal, use mixed sliced vegetables instead of chicken

10 to 12 spring roll wrappers (or use filo pastry sheets cut into 20 cm squares)

SPRING ROLL FILLING

250 g chicken breasts, skinned and thinly sliced

6 spring onions, finely diced

200 g fresh bean sprouts

3 dried Chinese mushrooms, soaked in hot water for 30 minutes; thinly slice caps, discard stems

MARINADE

1 tablespoon salt-reduced soy sauce

2 tablespoons Chinese wine or sherry

2 teaspoons finely chopped fresh ginger root

2 cloves garlic, finely chopped

freshly ground black pepper

1 fresh red chilli, chopped and seeds removed

SAUCE

1 tablespoon basic Chinese chicken stock (see recipe page 64)

1 tablespoon Chinese wine or dry sherry

2 teaspoons cornflour mixed with 1 tablespoon cold water

1 Preheat oven to 200°C (400°F).

2 Combine marinade ingredients and marinate chicken for 15 minutes.

3 Add chicken to a preheated wok or frypan and stir-fry for 2 to 3 minutes. Add spring onions, bean sprouts and mushrooms and stir-fry for 2 minutes.

4 Mix sauce ingredients together. Add to wok and stir until sauce thickens. Allow mixture to cool. Drain off excess liquid.

5 Divide mixture into 10 to 12 portions and place 1 portion in centre of spring roll wrapper. Fold sides over and roll up into parcel. Bake in oven for 30 minutes until golden brown. Serve with a dipping sauce (See recipes for more sauces on page 75).

SERVES 4 TO 6

BUDDHIST MUSHROOMS

115 g dried Chinese mushrooms, soaked in hot water for 30 minutes; cut caps into quarters, discard stems

115 g field mushrooms, sliced, discard stems

220 g straw mushrooms, rinsed and drained

2 teaspoons finely chopped, fresh ginger root

3 spring onions, finely chopped

3 tablespoons basic Chinese vegetable stock (see recipe page 64)

2 tablespoons Chinese wine or dry sherry

1 tablespoon low-salt soy sauce

2 teaspoons cornflour

1 teaspoon ground pepper

1 In a non-stick frypan, stir-fry all mushrooms with ginger and spring onions in 2 tablespoons stock for 3 minutes.

2 Combine remaining stock, wine and soy sauce with the cornflour. Add to mushrooms, reduce heat and simmer for 2 minutes. Season with pepper and serve.

SERVES 4 TO 6

FISH WITH MANGOES

¼ cup (60 ml) basic Chinese chicken or vegetable stock (see recipe page 64)

1 teaspoon finely chopped, fresh ginger root

1 teaspoon garlic, finely chopped

500 g fish fillets, skinned and cut into slices

3 fresh ripe mangoes, sliced

SAUCE

1 tablespoon cornflour

1 cup (250 ml) fresh orange juice

1 tablespoon salt-reduced soy sauce

1 tablespoon Chinese wine or dry sherry

freshly ground black pepper

1 Bring stock to the boil and stir-fry ginger and garlic for 1 minute.

2 Add fish pieces and stir-fry for 4 minutes. Remove from heat.

3 TO MAKE SAUCE: Combine cornflour with orange juice. Add remaining sauce ingredients. Bring to the boil in a small saucepan. Reduce heat and simmer, stirring, for 2 minutes or until sauce thickens.

4 Return fish to wok or frypan. Heat through and pour sauce over fish. Top with sliced mangoes and serve.

SERVES 4 TO 6

STEAMED WHOLE CRAB

2 medium-sized crabs

MARINADE

2 tablespoons Chinese wine or dry sherry

1 tablespoon finely chopped, fresh ginger root

3 cloves garlic, finely chopped

2 teaspoons salt-reduced soy sauce

3 spring onions, chopped

1 Remove the hard top shells from crabs and chop each crab into 6 pieces. Remove inedible portions. Chop off claws and crack shell with back of Chinese chopper. Break legs into pieces.

2 Place crab pieces in a deep heatproof bowl. Combine marinade ingredients, pour over crab pieces and marinate for 30 minutes.

3 Transfer heatproof bowl to bamboo steamer and steam vigorously for 10 to 15 minutes. Serve immediately.

SERVES 4 TO 6

✐ CHINESE MUSHROOMS

Always choose the thick black variety of Chinese mushrooms. Soak them in warm stock or water for 20 minutes to soften. Retain stalks for stocks. Chinese mushrooms can be stir-fried, braised, steamed, chopped and added to rice and poultry stuffings. Store them in an airtight jar.

*Steamed Whole
Szechuan Fish*

STEAMED WHOLE SZECHUAN FISH

3 dried Chinese mushrooms

750 g whole fresh fish (whiting, perch or snapper)

3 spring onions, chopped

1 tablespoon finely chopped, fresh coriander, for garnish

SAUCE

1 tablespoon finely chopped, fresh ginger root

2 fresh red chillies, sliced

1 tablespoon salt-reduced soy sauce

2 tablespoons vinegar

2 tablespoons Chinese wine or dry sherry

freshly ground black pepper

1 Soak mushrooms in hot water for 30 minutes, halve caps and discard stems.

2 Place fish on heatproof plate and sprinkle with spring onions and mushrooms.

3 Combine sauce ingredients and pour over fish. Steam for 10 to 15 minutes until fish flesh is white and flakes. Garnish with fresh coriander.

SERVES 4 TO 6

STEAMED GINGER PRAWNS

300 g fresh uncooked (green) prawns, shelled and deveined

1 tablespoon finely chopped, fresh coriander for garnish

MARINADE

2 tablespoons finely chopped, fresh ginger root

2 teaspoons salt-reduced soy sauce

2 tablespoons Chinese wine or dry sherry

2 cloves garlic, chopped

¼ teaspoon Chinese five spice powder

1 Mix marinade ingredients and marinate prawns for 30 minutes.

2 Place on a heatproof dish. Transfer to a bamboo steamer and steam vigorously for 7 to 8 minutes. Serve hot or cold garnished with fresh coriander.

SERVES 4 TO 6

STIR-FRIED SQUID WITH BROCCOLI

500 g squid, washed and cleaned

¾ cup (185 ml) basic Chinese chicken stock (see recipe page 64)

1 tablespoon finely chopped, fresh ginger root

2 cloves garlic, chopped

300 g broccoli, sliced diagonally

2 red capsicums, cut into thin strips

2 teaspoons cornflour

1 tablespoon salt-reduced soy sauce

2 tablespoons Chinese wine or dry sherry

4 spring onions, diced

1 Slit squid body lengthways and lay out flat. With a sharp knife make shallow cuts on the inside in a crosshatch diamond pattern. Cut the squid into 4 cm squares.

2 In a wok or frypan, combine 2 tablespoons chicken stock, squid, ginger and garlic and stir-fry over high heat for 2 minutes. Remove squid.

3 Add broccoli, capsicum and another 2 tablespoons stock to the wok and stir-fry over low heat for 3 minutes.

4 Mix together cornflour, remaining stock, soy sauce and wine. Add to wok, bring to the boil and simmer for 1 minute.

5 Return squid, add spring onions and simmer until heated through. Serve hot.

SERVES 4 TO 6

Stir-fried Squid with Broccoli

STEP-BY-STEP TECHNIQUES

Stir-fry chicken in marinade for 3 minutes.

Add vegetables and stir-fry for 2 minutes.

Add sauce to chicken and vegetables and simmer until sauce thickens.

CHICKEN WITH SNOW PEAS AND CAPSICUM

400 g chicken breasts, shredded

200 g snow peas, stems removed and trimmed

1 red capsicum, cut into strips

1 yellow capsicum, cut into strips

1 large carrot, cut into strips

MARINADE

1 tablespoon finely chopped, fresh ginger root

3 cloves garlic, chopped

1 tablespoon salt-reduced soy sauce

2 tablespoons Chinese wine or dry sherry

1 teaspoon cornflour

1 teaspoon ground cumin

1 teaspoon crushed red chillies

freshly ground black pepper

3 tablespoons basic Chinese chicken stock (see recipe page 64)

SAUCE

2 teaspoons cornflour

4 tablespoons basic Chinese chicken stock

1 tablespoon Chinese wine or dry sherry

1 Combine marinade ingredients and marinate chicken for 15 minutes.

2 Place chicken and marinade in heated wok and stir-fry for 3 minutes. Add vegetables and stir for 2 minutes.

3 TO MAKE SAUCE: Mix cornflour with stock and wine. Add to chicken and vegetables. Simmer, stirring continuously, for 2 minutes until sauce thickens. Serve immediately.

SERVES 4 TO 6

RED-COOKED CHICKEN

1½ kg chicken, skinned

2 tablespoons chopped, fresh ginger root

1 cup (250 ml) salt-reduced soy sauce

1 cup (250 ml) Chinese wine or dry sherry

2 teaspoons Chinese five spice powder

3 cloves garlic, chopped

3 cups (750 ml) water

lemon wedges and parsley, for garnish

1 Truss chicken and place all ingredients in a large saucepan. Bring to the boil, reduce heat and simmer for 30 minutes. Baste chicken during cooking. Turn heat off and allow chicken to cool in liquid.

2 Remove chicken and chop into 16 to 20 pieces. Arrange pieces attractively on a platter, garnish with lemon wedges and parsley, and serve as a cold entrée.

SERVES 4 TO 6

PINEAPPLE CHICKEN WITH TANGERINE PEEL

1½ kg chicken pieces, skinned

2 tablespoons chopped, fresh ginger root

4 tablespoons dried tangerine peel, soaked in hot water for 20 minutes and drained

3 tablespoons chopped, fresh pineapple

2 tablespoons salt-reduced soy sauce

1 cup (250 ml) basic Chinese chicken stock (see recipe page 64)

2 tablespoons Chinese wine or dry sherry

freshly ground black pepper

1 Preheat oven to 180°C (350°F).

2 Place all ingredients in a casserole dish and cover. Cook for 30 minutes. Remove cover and cook for a further 10 minutes. Serve hot.

SERVES 4 TO 6

CHINESE CHICKEN WITH PLUM SAUCE

1½ kg chicken pieces, skinned

sliced fresh plums

MARINADE

2 cloves garlic, finely chopped

1 teaspoon finely chopped, fresh ginger root

¾ cup (185 ml) Chinese wine or dry sherry

1 tablespoon salt-reduced soy sauce

½ cup (125 ml) basic Chinese chicken stock (see recipe page 64)

freshly ground black pepper

PLUM SAUCE

3 teaspoons cornflour

¼ cup (60 ml) fresh orange juice

1½ cups (375 ml) puréed fresh or unsweetened canned plums

2 teaspoons white vinegar

1 tablespoon unsweetened apple juice

½ fresh red chilli, finely chopped and seeds removed

1 Combine marinade ingredients and marinate chicken overnight in refrigerator or for at least 2 hours, before cooking.

2 Place chicken and marinade in a casserole dish, cover and cook at 200°C (400°F) for 30 minutes.

3 TO MAKE SAUCE: Mix cornflour with orange juice. Add to other sauce ingredients and bring to the boil. Reduce heat and simmer for 2 minutes until sauce thickens.

4 Arrange chicken pieces on a serving plate. Sauce can be poured over or used as a dipping sauce. Garnish with plum slices and serve.

SERVES 4 TO 6

≈ **RED COOKED CHICKEN**

Use the remaining liquid from this recipe as a base for soups or sauces.

LEMON CHICKEN

500 g chicken breasts, skinned and thinly sliced

fresh lemon slices, for garnish

MARINADE

2 teaspoons salt-reduced soy sauce

3 tablespoons basic Chinese chicken stock (see recipe page 64)

2 tablespoons Chinese wine or dry sherry

freshly ground black pepper

SAUCE

¼ cup (60 ml) fresh lemon juice

¾ cup (185 ml) fresh orange juice

½ teaspoon grated lemon zest

2 teaspoons cornflour mixed with 1 tablespoon cold water

1 Combine marinade ingredients and marinate chicken for 15 minutes.

Lobster with Black Bean Sauce

2 Combine all sauce ingredients and bring to the boil in a small saucepan. Reduce heat and simmer, stirring, for 2 minutes until sauce thickens. Set aside.

3 Bring marinade juices to the boil in a hot wok or frypan. Add chicken and stir-fry for 5 minutes until chicken is cooked.

4 Stir in lemon sauce and simmer for 1 minute. Garnish with lemon slices to serve.

SERVES 4 TO 6

STEAMED CHICKEN AND BROCCOLI

1½ kg chicken pieces, skinned

2 cups broccoli florets

3 dried Chinese mushrooms soaked in hot water for 30 minutes; cut caps into quarters, discard stems

4 spring onions, chopped

MARINADE

1 tablespoon salt-reduced soy sauce

1 tablespoon Chinese wine or dry sherry

1 tablespoon basic Chinese chicken stock (see recipepage 64)

2 teaspoons finely chopped, fresh ginger root

2 teaspoons cornflour

1 Marinate chicken pieces for 15 minutes.

2 Place marinated chicken in heatproof dish with marinade, broccoli and mushrooms on top. Steam vigorously for 35 minutes. Garnish with spring onions and serve.

SERVES 4 TO 6

BEEF IN BLACK BEAN SAUCE

500 g beef fillet, thinly sliced (partially freeze beef for easy slicing)

1 medium-sized white onion, chopped

2 cloves garlic, finely chopped

1 teaspoon finely chopped, fresh ginger root

1 cup (250 ml) basic Chinese chicken stock (see recipe page 64)

1 tablespoon black soya beans, soaked in cold water for 15 minutes, drained and mashed

2 tablespoons Chinese wine or dry sherry

2 green capsicums, cut in strips

1 tablespoon cornflour

1 tablespoon salt-reduced soy sauce

1 Stir-fry beef, onion, garlic and ginger in ½ cup (125 ml) stock over high heat for about 2 minutes or until tender.

2 Add black beans and wine to hot wok and stir-fry for 1 minute.

3 Add capsicums to wok and stir-fry for 1 minute.

4 Combine cornflour, soy sauce and remaining chicken stock and add to wok. Simmer about 1 minute until sauce thickens.

SERVES 4 TO 6

LOBSTER WITH BLACK BEAN SAUCE

3 cloves garlic, finely chopped

1 tablespoon black soya beans, soaked in cold water for 15 minutes, drained and mashed

2 fresh red chillies, finely chopped and seeds removed

4 tablespoons basic Chinese chicken stock (see recipe page 64)

500 g fresh uncooked lobster meat, chopped into bite-sized pieces

1 tablespoon chopped, fresh ginger root

4 spring onions, finely chopped

SAUCE

2 tablespoons basic Chinese chicken stock

2 tablespoons Chinese wine or dry sherry

1 teaspoon cornflour

freshly ground Szechuan pepper

1 In a hot wok or non-stick frypan, stir-fry garlic, black beans and chillies with 4 tablespoons stock for 1 minute.

2 Add lobster pieces, ginger and spring onions and stir-fry for a further 3 to 4 minutes until lobster is cooked.

3 Combine sauce ingredients and add to wok. Simmer for 2 minutes until sauce thickens. Serve hot.

SERVES 4 TO 6

CHINESE DIPPING SAUCES

These delicious dipping sauces are ideal accompaniments to spring rolls, Mongolian hot pot meals, vegetable crudites and many more. The fresh ingredients make these sauces especially tasty.

SOY/GINGER DIP

4 tablespoons salt-reduced soy sauce

1 tablespoon finely chopped ginger root

1 Combine and serve.

MAKES 125 ML

SOY/MUSTARD DIP

4 tablespoons salt-reduced soy sauce

1 tablespoon Dijon-style mustard

1 Combine and serve.

MAKES 80 ML

SOY/CHINESE WINE OR DRY SHERRY DIP

4 tablespoons salt-reduced soy sauce

1 tablespoon Chinese wine or dry sherry

1 Combine and serve.

MAKES 80 ML

SOY/SESAME DIP

4 tablespoons salt-reduced soy sauce

1 tablespoon sesame seeds, toasted

1 Combine and serve.

MAKES 80 ML

SOY/LEMON DIP

4 tablespoons salt-reduced soy sauce

1 tablespoon fresh lemon juice

1 Combine and serve.

MAKES 125 ML

SOY/PINEAPPLE DIP

4 tablespoons salt-reduced soy sauce

2 tablespoons unsweetened pineapple juice

1 Combine and serve.

MAKES 125 ML

CHINESE SAUCES

Avoid using prepared sauces such as plum, oyster, sweet and sour, lemon, black bean and chilli. You can easily make these sauces at home using fresh, natural ingredients.

Chinese Vegetable Crudites

SOY/CHILLI DIP

4 tablespoons salt-reduced soy sauce

1 fresh red chilli, finely sliced

1 Combine and serve.

MAKES 80 ML

CHINESE VEGETABLE CRUDITES

4 dried Chinese mushrooms

1 cup broccoli florets

1 cup cauliflower florets

2 carrots, cut into thin strips

1 cucumber, sliced

4 spring onion curls (see recipe)

6 radish roses (see recipe)

DIPPING SAUCE

2 cloves garlic, chopped

2 tablespoons chopped, fresh ginger root

¼ cup (60 ml) salt-reduced soy sauce

1 tablespoon sesame seeds, toasted

squeeze lemon juice

1 Presoak Chinese mushrooms in hot water for 30 minutes. Steam for 10 minutes and slice in half.

2 Arrange vegetables decoratively on serving plate.

3 Combine sauce ingredients and serve with vegetables.

SERVES 4 TO 6

BEIJING FRUIT SALAD

1 cup watermelon balls

1 cup honeydew melon balls

2 cups diced fresh pineapple or canned unsweetened pieces

1 cup kiwi fruit circles

1 cup diced apple

❧ BEIJING FRUIT SALAD

This delicious fruit salad can be made with any seasonal fruits.

2 cups fresh lychees

1 cup sliced fresh mango

2 teaspoons finely chopped, fresh ginger root

½ clove garlic, crushed (optional)

1 cup (250 ml) fresh orange juice

1 cup (250 ml) unsweetened pineapple juice

fresh rose petals and violets, for garnish

1 Combine all ingredients except garnish.

2 Chill before serving and garnish with rose petals and violets.

SERVES 4 TO 6

LEMON AND ORANGE TWISTS

1 Cut a lemon and orange into thin discs.

2 With a sharp knife cut disc through the middle up to white pith.

3 Pull both ends of disc until it twists and place on your favourite fish, meat, chicken or vegetable dishes.

SPRING ONION CURLS

1 Remove outer skin of spring onion and trim both ends. Slice the green end into brush-like strips.

2 Cut down about 2½ cm into the spring onion. Place in iced water for 10 minutes until the spring onion curls.

CARROT CUTOUTS

1 Peel carrots and cut into thin discs.

2 Use a special pastry animal cutter to press into carrot discs, or carve your own animal shapes with a sharp knife. Flower petal shapes are also attractive.

RADISH ROSES

1 Rinse radishes.

2 With a sharp knife, cut small petal shapes all round each radish, leaving attached at base.

3 Put in cold water until rose shape opens.

🍃 FRESH FLOWERS

Fresh rose petals, violets and other flowers can add an artistic touch to Chinese meals. They look especially beautiful as a garnish with fresh fruit.

Beijing Fruit Salad

VIETNAMESE DISHES

BEEF WITH BAMBOO SHOOTS

5 tablespoons chicken or vegetable stock

500 g beef fillet, sliced very thinly (partially freeze beef for easy slicing)

1 cup canned bamboo shoots, rinsed well, drained and sliced

5 spring onions, thinly sliced

3 cloves garlic, finely chopped

1 tablespoon Vietnamese fish sauce (nuoc mam)

1 tablespoon sesame seeds, lightly toasted

1 Bring 3 tablespoons stock to the boil, preferably in a wok. Add beef and stir-fry for 1 minute. Remove beef and stock from wok.

2 Bring remaining 2 tablespoons stock to the boil in the wok. Add bamboo shoots, spring onions and garlic and stir-fry for 3 minutes. Return beef and stock to wok.

3 Add fish sauce and stir-fry for a further 2 minutes.

4 Add sesame seeds and stir until well combined. Serve hot with brown rice.

SERVES 4 TO 6

WHITE-COOKED CARROTS WITH SWEET AND SOUR SAUCE

1½ cups (675 ml) basic Chinese vegetable stock (see recipe page 64)

5 carrots, thinly sliced

SAUCE

¼ cup (60 ml) vegetable stock

2 teaspoons vinegar

4 tablespoons fresh orange juice

2 tablespoons unsweetened tomato juice

2 tablespoons Chinese wine or dry sherry

1 tablespoon cornflour

1 Bring Chinese stock to the boil. Add carrots, cover and simmer for 10 minutes. Drain and transfer carrots to dish.

2 TO MAKE SAUCE: Combine sauce ingredients and bring to the boil. Reduce heat and simmer, stirring, for 2 minutes until sauce thickens. Spoon sauce over carrots.

SERVES 4 TO 6

STEAMED FISH AND MUSHROOMS

500 g fish fillets (ling or perch), cut into thick slices

8 dried Chinese mushrooms, soaked in hot water for 30 minutes and sliced, discard stems

1 tablespoon chopped, fresh ginger root

2 cloves garlic, finely chopped

4 spring onions, chopped

1 tablespoon Vietnamese fish sauce (nuoc mam)

100 g rice vermicelli, soaked in hot water for 20 minutes and drained

1 tablespoon chopped, fresh coriander

1 Place fish in a heatproof bowl and cover with the sliced mushrooms.

2 Combine remaining ingredients and pour over the fish and mushrooms.

3 Transfer bowl to a steamer. Cover and steam for 8 to 10 minutes.

SERVES 4 TO 6

VIETNAMESE FISH SAUCE (NUOC MAM)

The main flavouring ingredient in Vietnamese cooking is nuoc mam, a fermented fish sauce. It has a stronger flavour than Chinese soy sauce, enriched by the addition of chillies, garlic, lime juice and vinegar. Use it in minimal quantities, and dilute with water or lemon juice to lessen the saltiness. It is readily available from Asian stores.

CHICKEN AND LEMON GRASS

500 g chicken breasts, thinly sliced

3 cloves garlic, finely chopped

2 fresh red chillies, finely chopped and seeds removed

3 spring onions, finely chopped

2 stalks lemon grass, tender part only, finely chopped

freshly ground black pepper

2 tablespoons Vietnamese fish sauce (nuoc mam)

⅔ cup (160 ml) chicken stock

chopped fresh mint and coriander, chopped for garnish

1 Combine chicken, garlic, chillies, spring onions, lemon grass, pepper and fish sauce in a bowl and marinate for 30 minutes.

2 Add mixture to preheated wok and stir-fry for 5 minutes with 3 tablespoons chicken stock.

3 Reduce heat. Add remaining stock to wok and simmer for a further 10 minutes. Garnish with mint and coriander and serve hot.

SERVES 4 TO 6

PRAWN SOUP WITH RICE VERMICELLI

6 cups (1½ litres) fish stock

1 teaspoon grated lemon zest

4 ripe medium-sized tomatoes, roughly chopped

2 cloves garlic, finely chopped

1 tablespoon finely chopped, fresh ginger root

2 spring onions, chopped diagonally

1 tablespoon Vietnamese fish sauce (nuoc mam)

400 g uncooked (green) prawns, shelled and deveined

100 g rice vermicelli, soaked in hot water for 20 minutes and drained

freshly ground black pepper

1 tablespoon finely chopped, fresh coriander, for garnish

Beef with Bamboo Shoots

1 Bring fish stock to the boil in a large saucepan. Add lemon zest, tomatoes, garlic, ginger and spring onions. Reduce heat and simmer for 5 minutes.

2 Add fish sauce, prawns and rice vermicelli and simmer for a further 5 minutes.

3 Season with pepper and garnish with coriander.

SERVES 4 TO 6

CHRISTMAS CHEER
AND OTHER OCCASIONS

In this section, you will find easy, healthy recipes for barbecues and outdoor picnics, children's parties, school lunches, Christmas dinners, and sweet treats. Looking after the family and friends can be fun when you feed them with nutritious, delicious food that you know is good for them.

It is easy to eat a gourmet Christmas dinner without added fat, oil, salt or sugar. The main difference between a rich traditional meal and a low cholesterol feast is that you won't fall asleep over the plum pudding! Cook and enjoy: turkey with stuffing, roasted vegetables in succulent sauces, Christmas cake and superb steamed pudding.

Barbecues can be much more than sausages, chops and steaks. Fish, chicken, fruit and vegetables are also great barbecue food and once you have eaten a 'healthy' barbecue, you may have difficulty facing up to a plate of fatty meat and greasy onions.

Introduce healthy food to your children. You will be surprised how much so-called 'junk food' — potato chips, ice cream, pizza, cakes and biscuits — can be made using healthy ingredients. These recipes are great for parties or after-school munchies and weekend snacks.

Enjoy low cholesterol cooking in all areas for all occasions.

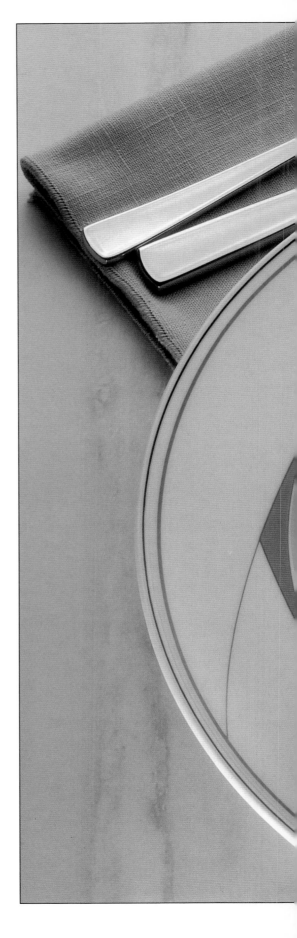

Christmas Turkey served with Herbed Roast Potatoes and Pumpkin, Stuffing, Peas and Cranberry Sauce

ROAST TURKEY

Roast turkey has half the fat and a third less cholesterol than roasted chicken. It is a good protein and iron source.

CHRISTMAS CHEER

CHRISTMAS TURKEY

1 Select a turkey that suits your Christmas lunch or dinner requirements.

2 Remove all skin before cooking.

3 Preheat oven to 200°C (400°F). Choose a tasty stuffing and place inside turkey. Do not pack stuffing tightly because it will expand considerably as the bird cooks.

4 Wrap turkey in foil. Place turkey in an ovenproof dish and bake for 30 minutes. Reduce oven temperature to 190°C (375°F). Bake a further 30 minutes. Remove foil and cook for another 30 minutes to brown and crisp the turkey. As rule, turkeys take 40 minutes per kilogram to cook.

5 Allow roasted poultry to stand for at least 15 minutes before carving. Instead of a greasy gravy, serve with a fresh fruit purée or chutney.

SAGE AND RAISIN STUFFING

½ cup cooked brown rice

½ cup homemade wholemeal breadcrumbs

1 tablespoon finely chopped, fresh sage or 2 teaspoons dried sage

1 tablespoon raisins, rinsed under cold water and drained

2 tablespoons fresh lemon juice

freshly ground black pepper

1 Combine all ingredients and stuff into cavity of chicken or turkey.

2 Truss or sew and bake in the oven.

PRUNE AND ONION STUFFING

1 cup homemade wholemeal breadcrumbs

1 medium-sized white onion, grated

8 pitted prunes, finely chopped

1 tablespoon fresh orange juice

1 tablespoon pine nuts (optional), lightly toasted

1 Combine all ingredients and stuff into cavity of chicken or turkey.

2 Truss or sew and bake in the oven.

HERBED ROAST POTATOES AND PUMPKIN

2 tablespoons fresh rosemary or 2 teaspoons dried rosemary

1 tablespoon chopped, fresh parsley

6 cloves garlic

freshly ground black pepper

2 kg potatoes, chopped

1 kg pumpkin, chopped into chunks

1 Preheat oven to 200°C (400°F).

2 Blend rosemary, parsley, garlic and pepper for a few seconds and set aside.

3 Bake potato chunks in a large ovenproof dish for 40 minutes.

4 Add pumpkin chunks beside potatoes in same dish and bake for a further 20 minutes.

5 Sprinkle with blended herb mixture and bake for a final 10 to 15 minutes.

SERVES 4 TO 6

MEXICAN RELISH

2½ kg extremely ripe tomatoes, finely chopped

½ cup (125 ml) white vinegar

1/4 cup finely chopped, fresh ginger root

12 cloves garlic, finely chopped

1½ cups (220 g) currants, rinsed under cold water and drained

1 cup grated green apple

2 tablespoons tomato paste

½ cup (125 ml) apple juice (not concentrate)

lots of freshly ground black pepper

1 Combine all ingredients in a large saucepan. Cover and simmer on gentle heat for 45 to 60 minutes. If there is too much liquid, remove lid for last 15 minutes cooking time to thicken.

2 Pour into jars and seal. Store in the refrigerator.

MAKES ABOUT 8 CUPS (2 LITRES)

BROCCOLI WITH CHEESE SAUCE

1½ kg broccoli florets, steamed for 5 minutes and set aside

SAUCE

2 cups ricotta or cottage cheese

3 cups (750 ml) skim milk

2 tablespoons grated Parmesan cheese

1 clove garlic, finely chopped

1 tablespoon chopped, fresh parsley

freshly ground black pepper

1 Blend sauce ingredients for a few seconds and place in saucepan. Heat through, but don't boil.

2 Pour over steamed broccoli and serve.

SERVES 4 TO 6

BEANS IN SAVOURY SAUCE

1 kg French green beans, cut into short lengths

SAUCE

1 kg very ripe tomatoes, chopped

1 tablespoon tomato paste

2 cloves garlic, finely chopped

1 heaped teaspoon mixed herbs

pinch paprika

¼ cup chopped, fresh parsley, to garnish

1 Steam or boil beans until tender. Set aside and keep warm.

2 Combine sauce ingredients, simmer for 15 minutes and pour over beans. Garnish with parsley and serve.

SERVES 4 TO 6

WARM CHRISTMAS RICE

1 cup (155 g) mixed dried fruit

1 tablespoon fresh lemon juice

¼ cup (60 ml) fresh orange juice

pinch cinnamon

6 cups cooked brown rice, keep warm

1 Combine fruit, juices and cinnamon in a pan. Simmer for 2 to 3 minutes, stir into rice and serve.

SERVES 4 TO 6

RICE

Neither brown rice or white rice contain any cholesterol. Brown rice has a slightly higher fat content but its dietary fibre makes it a lot healthier. Brown rice also contains more nutrients than white rice, such as iron, magnesium and zinc.

MEXICAN RELISH

This savoury dish is delicious served with roast chicken or turkey, rice, toast, or steamed vegetables.

Christmas Cake and Steamed Christmas Pudding

STEAMED CHRISTMAS PUDDING

1½ cups (290 g) pitted prunes

1½ cups homemade wholemeal breadcrumbs

1 cup (250 ml) unsweetened pineapple juice

1 cup (170 g) raisins

1 cup (155 g) currants

1 cup (155 g) mixed dried fruit

½ cup (60 g) chopped dried apricots

½ cup (90 g) sultanas

½ cup chopped, well-drained unsweetened pineapple pieces

grated zest 1 orange

grated zest 1 lemon

2½ cups (560 g) wholemeal self-raising flour

1½ teaspoons mixed spice

3 tablespoons brandy or Grand Marnier liqueur

1 Cover prunes with water, simmer for 5 minutes, and purée.

2 Combine breadcrumbs and pineapple juice, then add fruit and zest. Stir in flour, spice and brandy. Combine well. Pour into 2 litre pudding basin, lined with baking paper.

3 Place pudding basin into a large saucepan. Make sure water is at least halfway up side of pudding basin. Boil vigorously for 4 hours. Be careful not to let pan boil dry; add water progressively.

4 When cooked, carefully remove from basin and lining, wrap well in new foil or baking paper. Store in freezer or refrigerator.

5 On Christmas Day steam again for 2 hours. Serve with Ricotta Whip (see recipe) or low fat yoghurt.

SERVES 8 TO 10

RICOTTA WHIP

250 g fresh ricotta cheese

¼ cup (60 ml) skim milk

1 teaspoon vanilla essence

1 Blend all ingredients until smooth.

2 Serve as a topping for desserts. Delete vanilla essence and you have an instant creamy base for pasta sauces.

SERVES 4 TO 6

Step-by-Step Techniques

CHRISTMAS CAKE

1 cup sultanas

2 cups raisins

1 cup currants

1 cup mixed dried fruit

½ cup (125 ml) well-drained unsweetened pineapple pieces

½ cup pitted dates

1½ teaspoons mixed spice

2 teaspoons nutmeg

½ cup (125 ml) brandy

2½ cups (625 ml) fresh orange or unsweetened pineapple juice

juice ½ lemon

3 egg whites, stiffly beaten

3½ cups wholemeal self-raising flour, sifted

1 Preheat oven to 190°C (375°F).

2 Place fruit, spices, brandy, orange and lemon juices in a saucepan. Slowly bring to the boil. Reduce heat, cover and simmer for 5 minutes. Allow to cool.

3 Fold in egg whites and stir in flour.

4 Pour mixture into a 22 cm square or round non-stick tin, lined with baking paper. Cover top of cake with foil and bake for 1 hour. Remove foil and bake for a further 30 minutes. Allow to cool in tin. In warmer weather, store in refrigerator.

SERVES 8 TO 10

Bring to the boil fruit, spices, brandy, orange and lemon juices.

Fold in egg whites and stir in flour.

Pour mixture into a lined tin and bake.

To extract the best flavours, cook over hot coals not flames, and always preheat the barbecue for an hour before cooking begins. One-pot cooking is easy: try hearty soups and stews, a precooked vegetable, chicken or beef curry, or pasta. Marinate meat, fish or chicken the day before. Fresh herbs, wine and fruit juice preserve both food and flavour.

EATING OUTDOORS

THAI CHICKEN FRITTERS

6 chicken breasts, skin removed and trimmed of all visible fat and pricked with a fork

1 cup (125 g) wholemeal flour

3 egg whites, lightly beaten

MARINADE

6 spring onions

2 fresh red chillies

1 teaspoon chopped, fresh ginger root

4 cloves garlic

1 bunch fresh coriander, stalks discarded

½ teaspoon grated lemon zest

1 Blend marinade ingredients, spoon over chicken breasts and marinate for at least 2 hours.

2 Dip chicken into flour, then egg whites and barbecue on hot plate until tender, 10 to 12 minutes. Serve with brown rice and salad.

SERVES 4 TO 6

PEPPERY PUMPKIN SOUP

8 cups (2 litres) chicken or vegetable stock

2 kg pumpkin, cut into small chunks

2 teaspoons freshly ground black pepper

1 tablespoon finely chopped, fresh rosemary or 1 teaspoon dried rosemary

¼ cup (60 ml) low fat yoghurt

1 Place stock and pumpkin pieces in a large saucepan. Bring to the boil, cover and simmer for 20 minutes.

2 Stir in pepper and rosemary. Simmer for a further 5 minutes, then mash. Swirl through yoghurt and serve.

SERVES 4 TO 6

WHOLEMEAL CHIVE DAMPER

2 cups wholemeal self-raising flour

¾ cup (185 ml) skim milk

¼ cup chopped chives

freshly ground black pepper

1 Preheat oven to 200°C (400°F).

2 Sift flour and pour in milk. Combine well.

3 Add chives and sprinkle with pepper. Knead on a lightly floured board for a few minutes and mould into an oval shape.

4 Brush top of damper with extra skim milk and bake for 20 minutes until brown.

SERVES 4 TO 6

GARLIC ROLLS

225 g cottage cheese

6 cloves garlic

1 tablespoon chopped, fresh parsley

1 tablespoon chopped chives

freshly ground black pepper

6 wholemeal rolls

1 Purée all ingredients, except rolls.

2 Cut rolls in half and spread with herb and cheese mixture.

3 Wrap in foil and heat through on barbecue for 15 minutes.

SERVES 4 TO 6

POTATO, CELERY AND RADISH SALAD

½ bunch celery, diced

2 teaspoons black mustard seeds

1 kg potatoes, steamed and diced

8 to 10 radishes, trimmed and chopped

1 cup (250 ml) low fat yoghurt

1 tablespoon skim milk

1 Preheat non-stick frypan. Add mustard seeds and cook until they pop.

2 Off the heat, combine all ingredients, chill and serve.

SERVES 4 TO 6

Wholemeal Chive Damper and Garlic Rolls

BEETROOT AND GREEN PEA SALAD

500 g cooked beetroot, diced

500 g fresh peas, steamed until tender

DRESSING

1 cup (250 ml) fresh orange juice

1 teaspoon red wine vinegar

2 teaspoons finely chopped, fresh mint

freshly ground black pepper

1 Combine beetroot with peas.

2 Combine dressing ingredients and pour over vegetables. Chill and serve.

SERVES 4 TO 6

BRUSSELS SPROUTS SALAD

1 kg small Brussels sprouts

DRESSING

2 spring onions, finely chopped

½ cup (125 ml) salt-reduced soy sauce

juice 1 lemon

juice 1 orange

2 teaspoons sesame seeds, toasted

1 Steam Brussels sprouts until tender.

2 Combine dressing ingredients, pour over sprouts, chill and serve.

SERVES 4 TO 6

🥬 BRUSSELS SPROUTS

These are best in winter though available all year. They should be firm and bright green. Store in the refrigerator in a vegetable crisper for up to a week.

MARINATED MUSHROOMS

500 g button mushrooms, discard stems

MARINADE

2 tablespoons fresh lemon juice

¼ cup (60 ml) fresh orange juice

1 teaspoon red wine vinegar

2 cloves garlic, minced

1 tablespoon finely chopped, fresh parsley

freshly ground black pepper

1 Marinate mushrooms overnight or for at least 2 hours. Barbecue for 5 minutes, serve.

SERVES 4

HONIARA MARINATED FISH

1 kg firm fish fillets, cut in thick chunks

MARINADE

½ bunch fresh parsley, chopped and stalks removed

1 cup (250 ml) dry white wine

2 tablespoons fresh lime juice

1 medium-sized white onion, sliced

1 cup fresh pineapple pieces, puréed

freshly ground black pepper

1 Marinate fish overnight.

2 Barbecue until fish flakes with a fork. Baste during cooking.

SERVES 4 TO 6

CRISPY CALAMARI

1 kg calamari tubes, rinsed, drained and cut into thin rings

MARINADE

1 cup (250 ml) fresh lemon juice

½ cup chopped, fresh parsley

1 tablespoon wholemeal flour

6 cloves garlic, minced

¼ cup (60 ml) dry white wine

freshly ground black pepper

1 Combine marinade ingredients and marinate calamari overnight or for at least 2 hours.

2 Place on barbecue hot plate or grill and cook for 4 to 6 minutes until crisp. Serve with salad.

SERVES 4 TO 6

CHILLI PRAWNS

1 kg uncooked (green) prawns, shelled and deveined, tails left on

MARINADE

1 fresh green chilli

1 fresh red chilli

1 bunch fresh coriander

½ cup finely chopped, fresh mint

6 cloves garlic

juice 4 limes

freshly ground black pepper

1 Blend marinade ingredients and marinate prawns for at least 2 hours.

2 Barbecue on hot plate or grill for 8 to 10 minutes.

SERVES 4 TO 6

ROSEMARY CHICKEN FILLETS

1 kg chicken fillets, trimmed of any visible fat

MARINADE

1 tablespoon finely chopped, fresh rosemary or 1 teaspoon dried rosemary

2 cloves garlic, finely chopped

juice 1 orange

1 cup (250 ml) dry white wine

freshly ground black pepper

1 Combine marinade ingredients and marinate chicken overnight. Barbecue until tender, basting with marinade during cooking. Serve with salad.

SERVES 4 TO 6

SIZZLING BEEF WITH BARBECUE SAUCE

1 kg beef fillet, trimmed of all visible fat and diced

BARBECUE SAUCE

1 cup (250 ml) red wine

½ cup (125 ml) fresh orange juice

4 cloves garlic, finely chopped

1 teaspoon red wine vinegar

1 tablespoon tomato paste

1 teaspoon paprika

1 teaspoon chopped, fresh parsley

freshly ground black pepper

1 Combine sauce ingredients, place in a saucepan and bring to the boil. Reduce heat and simmer for 3 to 4 minutes.

2 Place diced beef on barbecue hot plate. Baste with sauce and sizzle until tender, 10 to 15 minutes. Pour over any remaining sauce and serve with salad.

SERVES 8 TO 10

DELICIOUS JACKET POTATOES

TOPPING 1

1 tablespoon finely chopped, fresh parsley

1 tablespoon grated Parmesan cheese

freshly ground black pepper

TOPPING 2

1 fresh red chilli, minced

1 clove garlic, minced

1 teaspoon finely chopped, fresh ginger root

TOPPING 3

1 tablespoon finely chopped, fresh coriander

1 tablespoon low fat yoghurt

dash grated lemon zest

freshly ground black pepper

TOPPING 4

1 tablespoon fresh lemon juice

1 tablespoon grated white onion

1 teaspoon finely chopped, fresh mint

TOPPING 5

1 tablespoon fresh tomato purée

¼ teaspoon hot paprika

1 teaspoon finely chopped chives

Honiara Marinated Fish, Delicious Jacket Potatoes and Marinated Mushrooms

1 Prepare 2 to 3 medium-sized potatoes per person, depending on how much other food is being served.

2 Sprinkle potatoes with 1 tablespoon of one of the above zesty combinations.

3 Wrap in foil and bake over hot coals for 1 to 1½ hours. Test with a metal skewer to ensure potatoes are cooked.

*Bad eating habits are
hard to break, so why not
introduce healthy food to
your children before they
become addicted to fat,
sugar and salt? General
irritability, fatigue and
even tantrums can be
induced by a poor diet.*

ESPECIALLY FOR KIDS

FRUIT KEBABS

3 bananas, chopped

250 g punnet strawberries

1 bunch grapes

1 ripe pineapple, thickly diced

6 apricots, halved

3 green apples, chopped

1½ cups (375 ml) fresh orange juice

1 Thread fruit pieces in an attractive order
on to metal or pre-soaked bamboo skewers.
2 Barbecue for a few minutes, basting with
orange juice during cooking.

SERVES 4 TO 6

SPICY VEGETABLE KEBABS

**200 g vegetables per person (zucchini
slices, capsicum slices, celery pieces, cherry
tomatoes, small onions, small chunks of
pumpkin, carrot slices)**

MARINADE

1 cup (250 ml) low fat yoghurt

2 cloves garlic, minced

1 teaspoon finely chopped, fresh ginger root

1 tablespoon finely chopped, fresh coriander

freshly ground black pepper

1 Combine marinade ingredients and
marinate vegetables for at least 1 hour.
2 Thread on to metal or pre-soaked bamboo
skewers. Barbecue for 5 minutes and serve
with brown rice.

SERVES VARY

HEALTHY BURGERS

2 medium-sized zucchini (courgettes)

1 medium-sized carrot

1 small onion

1 capsicum (pepper)

1 very ripe small tomato

**500 g lean minced beef or cooked
mashed potato**

freshly ground black pepper

2 egg whites

1 tablespoon chopped, fresh parsley

1 cup homemade wholemeal breadcrumbs

1 Chop and blend all vegetables until fine.
2 Add to meat, or potato, with pepper, egg
whites, parsley and breadcrumbs. Form into
small patties.
3 Preheat a non-stick frypan on high and
cook on both sides for 5 to 6 minutes.
4 Serve between Pritikin wholemeal rolls
with salad of your choice — alfalfa sprouts,
tomato slices, shredded lettuce or cabbage
— and tomato sauce or chutney.

SERVES 4 TO 6

EASY VEGETARIAN PIZZA

1 piece wholemeal pita bread

SAUCE

3 very ripe medium-sized tomatoes

1 small onion, finely diced

**1 red or green capsicum (pepper), cut into
rings or strips**

**1 medium-sized zucchini (courgette),
thinly sliced**

1 small carrot, grated

1 cup unsweetened pineapple pieces

1 Preheat oven to 200°C (400°F).
2 Purée tomatoes and onion and spread
mixture over pita bread. Sprinkle with other
ingredients. Bake for 15 minutes, slice
and serve.

SERVES 4

BANANA HOT DOGS

4 slices fresh wholemeal bread

2 tablespoons mashed ricotta cheese

1 teaspoon sesame seeds, lightly toasted

4 ripe bananas

1 Spread bread slices with ricotta cheese. Sprinkle with sesame seeds.

2 Enclose peeled banana, roll up and serve to the nearest child saying: 'I'm hungry!'

SERVES 4

CELERY SHARKS

1 bunch celery

2 large carrots, peeled

500 g ricotta or cottage cheese

1 Remove celery strings and cut stalks into short lengths.

2 Slice carrots into thin discs and cut out orange triangles.

3 Stuff cheese into celery lengths. Put carrot triangle (fins) into cheese.

4 Cover serving platter with blue cellophane paper to resemble the ocean. Arrange celery on top and serve.

SERVES 4 TO 6

REAL POTATO CHIPS

6 medium-sized potatoes

1 Preheat oven to 200°C (400°F).

2 Slice potatoes thinly with a potato peeler. Place in iced water in freezer for 5 minutes. Drain and pat dry.

3 Bake in a non-stick oven dish for 15 to 20 minutes until brown.

SERVES 4 TO 6

GREEN RICE SALAD

6 cups cooked brown rice

1 cup lightly steamed broccoli florets

3 spring onions, finely chopped

½ cup diced celery

½ cup boiled or steamed fresh peas

1 tablespoon chopped, fresh parsley

¼ cup (60 ml) fresh orange juice

freshly ground black pepper

1 Combine all ingredients and serve.

SERVES 4 TO 6

BANANA RAISIN MILKSHAKE

1 ripe banana

1 cup (250 ml) skim milk

1 tablespoon raisins, rinsed under cold water and drained

1 tablespoon low fat yoghurt

1 Combine all ingredients and blend until frothy.

SERVES 1 TO 2

Fruit Kebabs and Spicy Vegetable Kebabs

*Healthy Burgers and
Strawberry Milkshakes*

SPICY OAT LOAF

This should be stored in the fridge to keep it fresh

3 cups (270 g) raw oats

**3 cups (500 g) mixed dried fruit, rinsed
under cold water and drained**

1 teaspoon mixed spice

1 tablespoon baking powder

¼ cup (60 ml) low fat yoghurt

¼ cup (60 ml) apple juice concentrate

1 cup (250 ml) skim milk

1 teaspoon vanilla essence

1 Preheat oven to 190°C (375°F).

2 Blend oats in food processor until they
become fine flour.

3 Make a well in the centre of the oat flour
and pour in all other ingredients.

4 Mix thoroughly and pour into a 28 cm
x 10 cm non-stick loaf tin. Bake for 35 to
40 minutes. Place on wire rack to cool. Wrap
in foil. Refrigerate overnight before eating.

SERVES 6 TO 8

STRAWBERRY MILKSHAKE

1 cup ripe strawberries, hulled

1½ (375 ml) cups skim milk

1 tablespoon low fat yoghurt

dash cinnamon

1 Combine all ingredients and blend until
frothy.

SERVES 2

MUESLI BARS

1½ cups (250 g) mixed dried fruit

1½ cups (135 g) raw oats

**¼ cup sesame seeds, toasted in a
non-stick frypan**

½ cup (250 ml) skim milk

1 egg white, lightly beaten

1 Preheat oven to 190°C (375°F).

2 Rinse dried fruit well, drain and pat dry
with clean towel.

3 Combine all ingredients and knead
mixture together with your hands.

4 Press into flattish square or oblong shape
on a non-stick baking tray.

5 Bake for 20 minutes. Cut into bars while
still warm. Refrigerate and serve.

SERVES 4 TO 6

PARADISE DESSERT

3 ripe mangoes

pulp from 5 passionfruit

1 tablespoon apple juice concentrate

2 tablespoons low fat yoghurt

4 oranges, peeled and thinly sliced

1 Blend mango flesh, passionfruit, apple
juice and yoghurt.

2 Pour mixture over oranges, chill and
serve.

SERVES 4 TO 6

PINEAPPLE CAKE

This is best eaten the day after baking it

3 cups (500 g) mixed dried fruit, rinsed under cold water and patted dry

1 cup (125 g) dried apricots, finely chopped

440 g unsweetened crushed pineapple

¼ cup (60 ml) sweet sherry or fresh orange juice

1 teaspoon mixed spice

1 teaspoon bicarbonate of soda

2 egg whites, stiffly beaten

2 cups (500 g) wholemeal self-raising flour, sifted

1 Line a 20 cm cake tin with baking paper and preheat oven to 150°C (300°F).

2 Combine dried fruits, pineapple, sherry and spice in a saucepan. Slowly bring to the boil, reduce heat and simmer for 5 minutes.

3 Cool, then add soda and egg whites. Mix in flour until well combined.

4 Pour mixture into prepared tin and bake for approximately 1¼ hours. Cool in the tin.

SERVES 6 TO 8

From left to right:
Spicy Oat Loaf,
Pineapple Cake and
Special Banana Cake

SPECIAL BANANA CAKE

½ cup (125 ml) cold water

1 cup (155 g) dates, pitted

25 g mixed peel, rinsed under cold water to remove excess sugar

150 g cottage cheese

3 very ripe bananas, mashed

3 egg whites, stiffly beaten

1½ cups (185 g) wholemeal self-raising flour, sifted

1 teaspoon bicarbonate of soda

1 tablespoon skim milk

1 Preheat oven to 180°C (350°F).

2 Place water, dates and mixed peel in a saucepan. Bring slowly to the boil. Reduce heat and simmer gently for 5 minutes. Cool.

3 Blend mixture with cottage cheese until smooth. Add bananas. Fold in egg whites and flour.

4 Dissolve soda in milk and slowly fold into the cake mixture.

5 Pour into a non-stick ring or loaf tin and bake for 45 minutes. Cool cake in tin for 5 minutes before turning out onto cake rack.

6 Allow to cool completely, then wrap in foil or baking paper and store in refrigerator.

SERVES 6 TO 8

🐚 BANANA CAKE

For a terrific treat to serve with afternoon tea, serve this very special cake with some low fat vanilla yoghurt and decorate with slices of fresh banana. Delicious and so healthy too!

MEASURING MADE EASY

HOW TO MEASURE LIQUIDS

METRIC	IMPERIAL	CUPS
30 ml	1 fluid ounce	1 tablespoon plus 2 teaspoons
60 ml	2 fluid ounces	¼ cup
90 ml	3 fluid ounces	
125 ml	4 fluid ounces	½ cup
150 ml	5 fluid ounces	
170 ml	5½ fluid ounces	
180 ml	6 fluid ounces	¾ cup
220 ml	7 fluid ounces	
250 ml	8 fluid ounces	1 cup
500 ml	16 fluid ounces	2 cups
600 ml	20 fluid ounces (1 pint)	2½ cups
1 litre	1¾ pints	

HOW TO MEASURE DRY INGREDIENTS

15 g	½ oz	
30 g	1 oz	
60 g	2 oz	
90 g	3 oz	
125 g	4 oz	(¼ lb)
155 g	5 oz	
185 g	6 oz	
220 g	7 oz	
250 g	8 oz	(½ lb)
280 g	9 oz	
315 g	10 oz	
345 g	11 oz	
375 g	12 oz	(¾ lb)
410 g	13 oz	
440 g	14 oz	
470 g	15 oz	
500 g	16 oz	(1 lb)
750 g	24 oz	(1½ lb)
1 kg	32 oz	(2 lb)

QUICK CONVERSIONS

5 mm	¼ inch	
1 cm	½ inch	
2 cm	¾ inch	
2.5 cm	1 inch	
5 cm	2 inches	
6 cm	2½ inches	
8 cm	3 inches	
10 cm	4 inches	
12 cm	5 inches	
15 cm	6 inches	
18 cm	7 inches	
20 cm	8 inches	
23 cm	9 inches	
25 cm	10 inches	
28 cm	11 inches	
30 cm	12 inches	(1 foot)
46 cm	18 inches	
50 cm	20 inches	
61 cm	24 inches	(2 feet)
77 cm	30 inches	

NOTE: We developed the recipes in this book in Australia where the tablespoon measure is 20 ml. In many other countries the tablespoon is 15 ml. For most recipes this difference will not be noticeable.

However, for recipes using baking powder, gelatine, bicarbonate of soda, small amounts of flour and cornflour, we suggest you add an extra teaspoon for each tablespoon specified.

USING CUPS AND SPOONS

All cup and spoon measurements are level

METRIC CUP			METRIC SPOONS	
¼ cup	60 ml	2 fluid ounces	¼ teaspoon	1¼ ml
⅓ cup	80 ml	2½ fluid ounces	½ teaspoon	2½ ml
½ cup	125 ml	4 fluid ounces	1 teaspoon	5 ml
1 cup	250 ml	8 fluid ounces	1 tablespoon	20 ml

OVEN TEMPERATURES

TEMPERATURES	CELSIUS (°C)	FAHRENHEIT (°F)	GAS MARK
Very slow	120	250	½
Slow	150	300	2
Moderately slow	160-180	325-350	3-4
Moderate	190-200	375-400	5-6
Moderately hot	220-230	425-450	7
Hot	250-260	475-500	8-9

INDEX